The ArtScroll Series®

HOUSE CALLS

by

Rabbi Yaakov and Hadassah Wehl

TO ETERNITY

The story of Dr. Selma Wehl, heroine
of medical practice and Torah living

Published by

Mesorah Publications, ltd

FIRST EDITION
First Impression . . . December 1987

Published and Distributed by
MESORAH PUBLICATIONS, Ltd.
Brooklyn, New York 11223

Distributed in Israel by
MESORAH MAFITZIM / J. GROSSMAN
Rechov Harav Uziel 117
Jerusalem, Israel

Distributed in Europe by
J. LEHMANN HEBREW BOOKSELLERS
20 Cambridge Terrace
Gateshead, Tyne and Wear
England NE8 1RP

ISBN:
0-89906-554-6 (hard cover)
0-89906-555-4 (paperback)

Printed in the United States of America by Noble Book Press Corp.
Bound by Sefercraft Quality Bookbinders, Ltd., Brooklyn, N.Y.

Dedicated

To the minds that thought

To the hearts that felt

To the legs that walked

To the hands that toiled

To Opi and Omi

ר׳ אהרן ב״ר יעקב שמואל ע״ה

ה׳ טבת תרמ״ט — י״ד אייר (פסח שני) תשד״ם

December 9, 1888 — May 16, 1984

האשה פרומט שרה בת הרב משה מרדכי ע״ה

כ״ד תמוז תרנ״ח — ג׳ ניסן תשמ״ז

July 14, 1898 — April 2, 1987

With admiration, respect and love,

Your children, grandchildren

and great-grandchildren

✑§ Table of Contents

Foreword *by Rabbi David Cohen*   viii

An appreciation *by Rabbi Yaakov Fruchter*   ix

Introduction   x

Chapter 1 — From Where It All Stems   17

Chapter 2 — A New Country   26

Chapter 3 — A Loyal Daughter   36

Chapter 4 — The Man Behind the Scenes   40

Chapter 5 — A Shabbos Walk   52

Chapter 6 — Another Way of Celebrating Yom Tov   58

Chapter 7 — The Mitzvah of the Eighth Day   63

Chapter 8 — In Appreciation   66

Chapter 9 — Why Pediatrics   70

Chapter 10 — Medicine At Her Fingertips   76

Chapter 11 — Twenty-Four Hours on Call   85

Chapter 12 — Integrity At Its utmost   98

Chapter 13 — The Total Picture   104

Chapter 14 — One Of A Kind   111

Chapter 15 — The End Of An Era   119

Appendix — Letter from Rabbi Moshe Stern,
         Debrecener Rav   125
         Letter from Rabbi Yeruchem Olshin,
         Rosh Yeshivah, Beth Medrash Govoha   126

Foreword

She had many virtues, but the one that was dominant was her feeling of responsibility. That attribute manifested itself whether she cared for a patient or donated to a cause; whether she stayed up all night above the call of duty, or phoned a child's mother with a rebuke for not notifying her of the child's recovery or lack of improvement.

It was that yoke of responsibility that made her carry her medical bag on Shabbos with a *shinnui*, willing to walk many a mile to examine a sick child.

It was this feeling that compelled her to drive one hour to a patient who needed her services; and to ask patients of other doctors, who consulted with her in emergency situations when their own doctors were not available, to pay her not more than their doctor's regular fee, because she didn't want to "take advantage of them."

Responsibility breeds discipline, and whenever in doubt she always asked a *sheilah* of a *posek*. She had entry to Rav Aharon Kotler צ״ל, and many other *Gedolei Yisrael* were impressed with her capabilities as a doctor, as well as with her *yiras hachet* (fear of transgressing the Torah's laws) and *midas hachessed* (lovingkindness).

She was feared and loved — feared by those who were irresponsible and whose insufficiencies or laxities would readily be detected by her, and loved by her patients over whom she doted. She was admired and respected. Indeed, some of her colleagues were in awe of her gifts of intellect and indefatigability. She demonstrated those qualities when she came to the United States as an impoverished woman who was an accomplished medical doctor but lacked certification to practice in this country. She worked diligently to earn her license and gain broad acceptance in the Boro Park community.

Throughout her career — as a great physician and as an exemplary *bas Yisrael* — she was a model of service to others, of devotion to Torah and its students, and of personal adherence to the observance of *mitzvos*. Though her husband, Reb Aharon, was a modest, humble man who preferred the background, he too was a Jew who won the respect of all who knew him. Their brand of wholesome *emunah* should be a model for succeeding generations. May this book be an inspiration, as they were in life.

Rabbi David Cohen
Rav D'BM Gevul Yavetz

An Appreciation

It is said that institutions come and go, meaning that many organizations or causes — once they have fulfilled their *raison d'etre* — will tend to fade from the scene, leaving no significant impact upon mankind.

But what if the "institution" was a human being, who during her lifetime left an indelible impression upon all who came in contact with her — what effect does such an "institution" leave upon us when it ceases to function and is gone from this earth? Does it also disappear? No! Certainly not!

At first its cessation turns into an אֲבֵלוּת דְּרַבִּים, *a period of public mourning.* As time goes on, it turns into a legacy and in the case of Dr. Selma Wehl, ע"ה, her life's work also becomes a book of *mussar*, of ethical and moral teaching.

It is almost a year since Dr. Selma Wehl passed away on 3 Nissan 5747, yet it is still difficult to accept the reality that our doctor, our friend, our "institution", no longer functions. It is hard to imagine that her office at 5015-15th Avenue, Brooklyn, no longer pulsates with the sounds of crying infants, that it is silent after forty-five years of constant service to the community — day and night — at all hours — in rain and snow — during old age and illness. Whenever she was needed she was ready: literally a one-woman institution, in which the words of our Sages; כָּל הַמְקַיֵּם נֶפֶשׁ אַחַת מִיִּשְׂרָאֵל . . ., *whoever saves one Jewish life . . .*, was not merely a saying, but a way of life.

This book relates many episodes and stories in the life of Dr. Selma and Mr. Aharon Wehl ע"ה — the good times and the hard ones; their *emunah* and *bitachon* (faith and trust in HASHEM) and unending and unselfish devotion to and compassion for her patients. From the unadorned story of her life, we see the tremendous סִיַּעְתָּא דִשְׁמַיָּא, *heavenly assistance* she had as a renowned pediatrician and diagnostician.

But the Wehls not only built an "institution" for others, they were also privileged to see the external reward in their lifetime:

— a home steeped in sanctity and vibrating with Torah study,

— generations steeped in devotion to Torah and *mitzvos*,

— thousands of patients who became *roshei yeshivah*, successful and productive members of communities and parents of new Torah generations,

— the satisfaction of seeing people alive today with HASHEM'S help because she was the Divine agent to save them.

The Wehl's earned the admiration of many of the greatest Torah luminaries of their generations.

Our human "institution", the legacy of our beloved Dr. Selma Wehl, has not faded away. It has gone from "House Calls to Eternity".

A grateful patient,
Rabbi Yaakov Fruchter

Introduction

Our Sages tell us that the obligation of honoring one's parents does not end with their passing away from this world: מכבדן בחייו ומכבדו במותו, *One is obligated to honor them in their lifetime; one is obligated to honor them after they have gone on to eternity.* (*Kiddushin* 31b)

Writing a book about one's own parents is a unique undertaking, for there is usually no one who really knows parents better than their own child. Yet our Sages have told us: לא קאי איניש אדעתי׳ דרבי׳ עד ארבעין שנין, *A person does not reach the ultimate understanding of what his Rebbe said until forty years thereafter* (*Avodah Zorah* 5b). Certainly within that framework, as less than six months have elapsed since our sainted mother has passed on, it is impossible to have a proper understanding of what our parents meant to us. On the other hand, it seems to me that the *Torah Temimah* (*Deut.* 29:3) explains the Sages statement in a slightly different manner. He says that when a student sits before his *Rebbe* for forty years, he will finally penetrate to the depths of his *Rebbe's* mind. In other words one needs a forty-year in-service period to reach into the depths of his *Rebbe's* mind. Homiletically, then, one might compare the above-mentioned forty-year period to the same span of years during the time of Moshe Rabbeinu, a time that the Jews traveled through a desert, with all the trials, tribulations and miracles that they saw.

Every *Rebbe* and every parent blazes a path for the new generation, and it is only when the new generation sees the whole trail completed that it can understand something of the desert of life. Missing one element of it curtails one's comprehension of events. Rabbi Shamshon Raphael Hirsch, in his classical commentary on the verses זכר ימות עולם בינו שנות דר ודר, *Remember the days of old, comprehend the years of the generations, ask your father, he will relate it to you, your elders will explain it to you, (Deut.* 32:7) explains: "Follow the path of the development of the generations of Man, and then ask your father about your own history, he will make it vividly realistic to you. Your elders who are gifted with wisdom and insight, they will explain your history to you; they will explain the connection between your origin and your mission to the world."

It is incumbent upon children and grandchildren to look back from time to time to see if they are following in the footsteps of those who preceded them. This is true for every single child in relation to his own ancestors. There are some people who not only transmitted their own personal customs and traditions but they personified in themselves a whole transitionary period. They represented a bygone era, an era that may never be seen again, For these people life was indeed a forty-year stay in the desert. They were exiled from their land of birth, they had to resettle in a new country, learn a new language, and start over again at an age when others are already dreaming of retirement. Despite all that, they remained true to their own background, not adjusting their values to the times, but instead, insisting that the times adjust to their values. It is these people who blazed a trail for their own individual families and were a beacon of light to their communities. They showed that Torah, when passed on in its purest form, without compromise, is bound to remain eternal. They became part of the historical background not only of their families but of the whole community as well. They demonstrated that the sanctity of the Giver of life, the Almighty above, can and should permeate every one of their actions in both their personal and professional lives.

In an interesting anecdote the *gemara (Bava Metzia* 85b) relates that Shmuel saw the *sefer* (book) of Adam, in which the Almighty had shown Adam all the forthcoming generations, their scribes and their Torah scholars. It was recorded in this *sefer* that he, Shmuel, would become the doctor of the sainted Rabbeinu Hakodosh. What an interesting phenomenon it is that, at the time of the master plan of creation, the role of the doctor of great people was already delineated! If one thinks about it, it is not difficult to understand. For as the famous *tefilas harofeh* (prayer for the doctor) attributed to the Rambam (Maimonides) states, "Just let the truth lead me because any deviation or compromise in my profession can bring destruction and illness to the creation of Your hand." Thus, the doctor is in a limited sense a partner or messenger to help the creations of Hashem's hand survive and flourish.

Those of us who had the privilege of knowing Mr. Aharon and Dr. Selma Wehl, who in this book will be referred to as Opi and Omi, (German terms of endearment for grandfather and grandmother) know that they personified this partnership. As Rabbi Fruchter, who chaired the *hesped* on the *sheloshim** for Omi, said, "Besides the everlasting reward that awaits her in the eternal world, she was privileged to see her efforts reach fruition in this world. She was able to see many generations of young men and women, some of whom are today's leading *roshei yeshivah* (deans of Talmudical seminaries), involved in the learning of Torah and the fulfillment of its commandments and precepts. She nurtured thousands of wives of *bnei Torah* as well as many fine religious lay leaders, and she felt inordinate satisfaction in knowing that she was instrumental in keeping children alive, with the help of the Almighty, acting as His *messenger*."

As we wrote this book we could not escape our own feelings of ineptness when it came to an understanding of our own parents. We beg their forgiveness. It is quite possible that they themselves, due to their humility, would have felt that this book should not have been written. Yet we know that there were no two people who regarded each other with such great esteem as they did. Thus, if each one of them is upset by the honor that is being given to him or her, we feel that it is compensated for by the honor or reverence that each of them felt that the other should receive. We hope that this book, for all its human frailties, will affect our everyday actions in a positive manner. May some of the remarkable anecdotes of the *midos* of our parents prompt us to stop for a moment and rethink some aspect of our lives. May it also bring about the desire to recall our own ancestral background, motivating us to strive to perpetuate that which was holy and sacred in their lives. Then we will have fulfilled at least to a degree the *mitzvah* of *kibud av v'em*, that of honoring our parents.

---

*Sheloshim — (a) Thirty-day mourning period (b) The day ending the thirty-day mourning period. Frequently marked by a memorial service where eulogies are given and often a *siyum mishnayos* (completion of the study of *mishnayos*) is rendered.

For as Rabbi Shlomo Ganzfried wrote: מי שהוא רוצה באמת לכבד את
אביו ואת אמו יעסוק בתורה ובמעשים טובים שזהו הכבוד הגדול להאבות
שאומרים הבריות אשרי לאב ואם שגדלו בנכזה, he who truly wishes to
honor his father and his mother should devote himself to the study of
the Torah and to the performance of good deeds, for this is the
greatest honor to his parents, because people will say, "Happy are
the parents who brought up such a child" (Kitzur Shulchan Aruch
143:21). May all of us strive to achieve that goal until the day that we
will be privileged to once again be reunited with them in the days of
techiyas hamasim (the awakening of the dead), upon the building of
the Beis HaMikdash (Holy Temple), bimherah beyamenu, Amen.

ACKNOWLEDGMENTS

An undertaking of this kind requires the encouragement and
cooperation of many. We gratefully acknowledge the many letters,
tape recordings and personal stories that helped make this book into
a reality.

Likewise we certainly record with thanks the extraordinary efforts
that were undertaken by RABBI YAAKOV POLLAK, the Rav of
Congregation Shomrei Emunah; RABBI SIMCHA BUNIM EHRENFELD, the
Matersdorfer Rav; RABBI GERSHON WEISS, the Menahel of Yeshivah of
Staten Island; RABBI YAAKOV FRUCHTER, Director of Publications of
Torah Umesorah, who contributed the foreword; and RABBI MARVIN
SCHICK, President of Yeshivah and Mesifta Rabbeinu Yaakov Yosef
(the Rabbi Jacob Joseph School), in presenting such eloquent
hespedim (eulogies). Much of what they have said has been
incorporated into this book.

From the time of her death and even years before, Rabbi Yaakov
Fruchter, himself a former patient, and a parent and grandparent of
patients, inspired and prodded us to write this book to educate future
generations. It is our hope that the midos (character traits),
self-sacrifice, and sincere Yiddishkeit depicted in this book may serve
as guideposts along the road of life.

The difficult task of editorially reviewing this book was undertaken by two very dear and devoted patients of Omi, MRS. DEVORAH
SCHECHTER and MRS. MALKAH SCHICK. They spent endless time
making this book more readable. During the time that the book was

in preparation it became a family mission for the Schechter and Schick households. May all the Schechter and Schick children continue to give much *nachas* to their parents and to Klal Yisrael. In addition our work was augmented by the expertise of MRS. AVIVA METCHIK. All of these worked on the book despite their heavy schedules in the field of *chinuch habanos*. May their work bear the fruit they so richly deserve. Likewise, we are indebted to DR. YEHUDAH MEIR SCHECHTER for his invaluable suggestions, among them his aid in choosing the title for this book.

A special thanks to one of the younger *Manhigei Hador* (leaders of our generation), RABBI DAVID COHEN. During the time that his children were Omi's patients, he and his Rebbetzin developed a close relationship with her. His foreword has certainly enhanced our book.

A number of individuals spent hours translating some of the German documents that had personal meaning to us. Not only did they provide the literal translation, but they attempted to maintain the spirit of that which was said. We acknowledge with thanks the efforts of DR. and MRS. ERNEST BODENHEIMER, as well as those of our cousin EVA COHEN, for their labors in this area.

Producing a book requires various drafts and certainly the use of a computer and word-processing material made the task a much simpler and more accurate one. For this we owe thanks to the administration of the Bais Yaakov of Boro Park.

As amateurs entering a new field we were constantly guided, advised and aided by the expert opinion and experience of RABBI NOSSON SCHERMAN. Not only was he acting in his capacity as the editor of the world famous ArtScroll series but also as a Boro Park resident, whose children and grandchildren benefited from Omi's expertise.

REB SHEAH BRANDER has manifested his talents, skills and efforts in presenting this book in such a beautiful and artistic manner.

RABBI AVIE GOLD has reviewed and edited the final manuscript, and supervised its preparation. We are thankful that his familiar stamp is on this book as on so many other ArtScroll volumes.

MRS. JUDI DICK, a long-time friend of the authors and a member of the ArtScroll staff, has enriched this book with her valuable suggestions. MRS. FAYGIE WEINBAUM has proofread the final draft.

In the words of the guiding spirit of ArtScroll, Rabbi Meir

Zlotowitz, "We consider it a privilege to collaborate in the dissemination of so beautiful and inspiring a book about so noble a figure." The Wehl family indeed considers it an honor to be included in the wonderful and outstanding literary contributions made by ArtScroll - Mesorah Publications. May Rabbi Scherman and Rabbi Zlotowitz continue to spread the words of Torah and Mussar through their outstanding publications.

We are grateful also to the typists who performed their work patiently, diligently, and cheerfully: MENUCHAH MARCUS, ZISSI GLATZER, and CHAVIE GLUCK. And we thank the other devoted and dedicated ArtScroll staff members for helping produce this wonderful book.

A personal thanks to our dear children and grandchildren who had to patiently bear with us while we were preoccupied with the publishing of this book. In addition, some of their suggestions have found their way into the text. But far above and beyond that go our feelings to them, for which there is no human ability to thank adequately, for having granted Opi and Omi so much *nachas* in their lifetime.

The greatest *hakoras hatov* (recognition for good) is due the Almighty above, Who gave us the kind of parents about whom a book could be written, Who rescued us from the burning furnaces of Europe to bring us to these shores, and Who enabled us to grow up under the guidance and influence of parents such as these. May they be a *malitz yosher* for us, our children, grandchildren, family, patients, friends and *klal Yisrael*.

Yaakov and Hadassah Wehl

CHAPTER I

From Where It All Stems

As we children began to undertake the task of writing a book about our sainted parents, we were fortunate to find a tape that our mother, Dr. Wehl, henceforth referred to as Omi, dictated herself. In the italicized paragraphs below, we have tried to maintain both the language and spirit of the tape. Thus much of the first chapters are written in a 'first-person' style. In her tape Omi mentioned that she was dedicating it to the memory of her parents, Rabbi Moshe Mordechai Lewin and Rebbetzin Lena Zuckerman Lewin, and to the memory of her life-long partner, Reb Aharon Arnold Wehl.

I was the oldest of three children, having a younger sister and brother. We were all brought up in a German rabbinical home in the small town of Wreschen, Posen. My mother, whose maiden name was Lena Zuckerman, was the daughter of Reb Moshe Ephraim Zuckerman, who sat and learned in the beis medrash (house of Torah study) the entire day.

My mother was a descendant of the famous Kalischer Rav and the great-granddaughter of the renowned Dayan of Obersitzko. The latter was privileged to have four responsa sent to him (and included in the works of) by Reb Akiva Eiger. Likewise her maternal grandfather, Rabbi Moshe Ephraim Zuckerman, spent all the days of his life in the beis medrash of Posen where he was reported to have served as dayan (judge) on the Jewish court.

By the time my father was twenty-seven years old, he had already received smichah (rabbinical ordination). He had learned in Prague under Rabbiner Ehrenfeld, and he had also attended the Rabbinical

Rabbi Moshe Ephraim Zuckerman

Seminary of Rabbi Hildesheimer in Berlin. That seminary was the leading rabbinical seminary for the preparation and ordination of Orthodox Rabbis in Germany. In addition he had received his Doctorate in the field of Aramaic Languages. He was proficient in Greek and Latin, which were to be a tremendous asset to me in my student years.

As a Rav in Wreschen, he served many small communities around him. He was a member of a study group of four rabbanim who met once a week to discuss the common problems facing them. In addition they would join in a study group to advance their Torah knowledge. After World War I, when the province of Posen became Polish, my parents moved to Hamburg and my father joined the staff of the Hamburg Talmud Torah school. This is comparable to our yeshivah elementary-high school here in America. To an extent, he continued functioning as a rav. He was a member of the Beis Din (Jewish Court) and on many occasions functioned as the emissary of the Chief Rabbi. In fact, when the position of Chief Rabbi of Hamburg became vacant he acted in that capacity for a period of two years.

Above all, our father had a heart of gold. He was the kindest person we knew.

This was not only felt by members of the family. Many years later on Opa Lewin's seventieth birthday he received the following letter from Oberrabbiner (Chief Rabbi) Carlebach, in which he writes: "I remember the many years we worked together, and recall your great accomplishments as a *Rav* in Wreschen. I remember, too, your continued fruitful work and labor in Hamburg. You can look back upon a full and enriched life. But above all, I remember the wonderful humane personality, our close relationship as colleagues and your great sense of modesty and humility. Your goodness to every single human being has caused you to be engraved in our hearts forever, and that will never leave us."

Omi was extremely proud of her father. She would always relate to us how as a young girl she was approached by a friend who boasted that her father was the richest man in town. Thereupon Omi answered, "But *my* father is the *Rav.*"

My mother lost her parents at the young age of seventeen. She was very perturbed by what she understood about the taharah (ritual

Farewell address by Rabbi Lewin (November 15, 1934 / 8 Kislev 5695) in the Kohlhöfenschul in Hamburg. The shul was destroyed a short time later.

preparation of a corpse prior to burial) of her mother. At that moment she made a commitment to become a member of the chevrah kadisha (burial society) when she would be mature enough to do so. As a young wife she often participated in a taharah. That was not her only act of chesed. In fact as children we were brought up with clear-cut instructions to make sure that everything was put away in its correct place each evening. We never knew if some poor person might become ill, in which case my mother herself, the Rebbetzin, would leave to spend the entire night with that family. Thus the house always had to be in order and ready for any eventuality. As Oberrabbiner Carlebach wrote in a letter to us after her petirah (death): "She was the crown of your house. We knew her especially well because we were neighbors. We always realized her piety. We noticed how lovely, nice and helpful she was to everybody. She was a true, sincere Rebbetzin. She had a good heart and toras chesed (a lesson of kindness) was always on her tongue." Growing up in such a home left an impact on us, the children, regarding the importance of serving and helping people in time of need and illness. It is not an accident, in trying to follow their example, that my siblings and I began entertaining the thought of medical and nursing careers. In fact, my sister Irma Froehlich ultimately became the administrator of a hospital here in the United States. My brother Ernst Ephraim became a dentist in Hamburg and later emigrated to Israel.

When I was five years old I started school. The teacher was frustrated because I did not seem to be able to learn the alphabet. Suddenly out of nowhere I discovered my brain and began reading the letters. From that time forward I became a very ambitious student. While other students were happy with the mark of 'B', if I received that mark I cried to such an extent that others thought I failed the course. I was satisfied with nothing less than an Excellent.

As already mentioned my father had gone through university and rabbinical school. His father died at an early age and thus he had to accomplish it all on his own. I felt that if my father could succeed at it so could his daughter.

A year or two after I finished high school, World War I broke out. I had already began tutoring in order to earn some money. Now circumstances provided me with an ideal opportunity. The Talmud Torah school teacher was drafted into the army, and my father was left to teach all the classes without any assistance. [Living on the Polish border, he had more duties than ever before. On one occasion he had to go to the army barracks to personally secure the release of the Jewish soldiers so that they could join the local shul for Yom Kippur.] The alternative became clear. I became the new Talmud Torah teacher. I did not get paid for this job. However as a reward, my father prepared me in Latin, Math, and English. I studied Chemistry and Physics on my own. I visited a college in the next city to find out the necessary requirements for a degree. I then planned my own home self-study program. My mother insisted that despite the time I was putting into my studies, I still had to be involved in the normal chores of a girl of those days, such as knitting, crocheting and sewing. These skills were not acquired in vain. To this very day I still enjoy knitting for my grandchildren and great-grandchildren.

During the war years I was influenced to a very large extent by observing an army physician and his sister, also a doctor, who served in our community. Even though I had always dreamed of being a doctor and was preparing my pre-med courses on a college level on my own, their practice of medicine inspired me to surge on to my goal.

In order to enter the university one had to pass a qualifying examination. This exam consisted of five written parts and one oral session. At the time of my application for this examination, I informed the Board of Examiners that I was a Sabbath observer. I told them that the part of the examination that was given on Friday would have to be finished early enough in order for me to board the train to reach home before the onset of Shabbos. After passing the final oral part of the examination, I traveled home. I was the first girl in the small city of Wreschen to pass such an examination. My father greeted me at the station with a warm welcome and with the permission that I would be able to study medicine. When my father was asked what advice he gave his daughter before she entered the university regarding her behavior, her observances of Shabbos, and her Yiddishkeit, he answered, "Eighteen years of education in a home with a strong background hopefully has taught her all that she needs to know."

Opa Lewin was expressing the German philosophy, based to a

large extent on the teachings of Rabbi Shamshon Raphael Hirsch, that one may combine *Torah Im Derech Eretz* — Torah jointly with the pursuit of worldly knowledge. Omi used to tell us that in Hamburg there were approximately three dozen religious doctors and dentists.

Our way of life in Germany was very rigid. Everyone only had two dresses, one for Shabbos and one for the weekdays. Of course these were sewn by my mother. Even in university all I possessed was two skirts, two blouses, and one pair of high-heeled shoes. I wasn't very excited about it, but I never asked for more.

I started my schooling in Breslau. There I had many friends, all of whom were religious. We formed a group for religious girls known as the Bruriah. It was at Breslau that I studied Anatomy. The course made such a deep imprint upon my mind that I recall writing a letter to my father suggesting to him that it is not possible to pursue the study of anatomy if one doesn't believe in the Almighty. One can work on a human corpse only if one understands that one is dealing with the external body and that the internal soul is exclusively associated with the Almighty.

In Breslau the chemical practicum was conducted only on Shabbos. You should all know that I never went to any lectures on Shabbos and yet I was the favorite student of the professor. He called me 'the green leaf'. When I couldn't answer one of his questions, he would say, "If the green leaf can't answer, what should the other students say?" Since the chemical practicum was on Shabbos I transferred to the University of Munich. In Munich I became very friendly with Bertha Ehrentrau, who was a diligent worker on behalf of Ezra and Bnos Agudath Yisrael.

After finishing the course in Munich, I returned to Breslau to begin preparing for my first qualifying examination as a physician. During my school years a major change had occurred in my hometown. The province of Posen, which had been part of Germany, had as a result of World War I became part of Poland. Our parents moved to Hamburg. This change had a great effect on my career. After Breslau I spent some time in Frankfurt am Main and I would have remained there had it not been for my parents' move to Hamburg.

Thereafter came my last two years in the study of medicine in the

Dr. Wehl as a student, surrounded by members of the Bruriah group she led.

field of Clinical Education. The State Boards had to be taken. Hamburg at that time was a relatively new university. I was the first religious student there. The examination in the area of surgery was scheduled for Shabbos. When I indicated to the professor that I could not work on a body to demonstrate my surgical skills because it was Shabbos, he failed me. He said, "What will you do in actual practice?" I explained that, in order to cure a living human being, a doctor is permitted to desecrate the Shabbos. Although I failed this test, a directive went out to all the professors at the Hamburg University that henceforth if any student refused to do work on Shabbos, due to religious reasons, such a student had to be freed from that requirement. I was the pioneer. I was strengthened by the episode despite the fact that I failed the subject.

After completing my clinical in-training period, I became a pediatrician. In 1928 I opened my office. It served the welfare group in Hamburg. As my practice developed and my reputation increased I opened another office in a second neighborhood, a suburb of Hamburg. In this part of town I had a very elegant office.

As time progressed our mother suddenly became gravely ill. My medical knowledge told me that there was very little we could do.

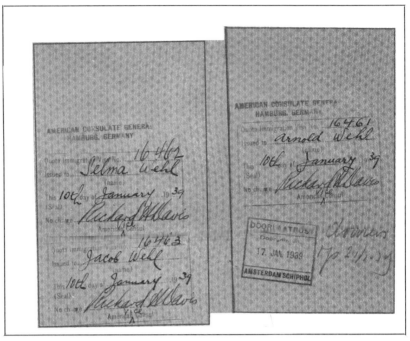

Quota Immigration Visa numbers 16461, 16462, 16463, assigned to the Wehls. This number was a prerequisite for admission into the United States.

After she passed away my sister and I remained with our father. At that time both of us began considering marriage. After my sister married Mr. Kurt Froehlich, I married my life partner, Reb Aharon Wehl in March 1936 (Adar 5696). When our son was born, we were very proud and happy people. Yet we were already living in the Nazi era. We could never walk out alone in the street. A member of the Gestapo would always be following us. People began leaving Germany even though many couldn't believe that the Nazis would actually kill the Jews. They felt it was just a passing frenzy.

My husband's sister, Dora, encouraged us to obtain a number from the American Embassy, and we followed her advice. America, at the time, had a quota system. Not everyone who wanted to enter the United States was allowed to do so. Thus a person interested in leaving Hamburg to go to America had to obtain a qualifying number from the United States consul in Hamburg. On a Shabbos morning the Gestapo came to call for my husband. Despite the fact that I fainted upon seeing them, they insisted on taking my husband away.

They told him to take his money with him. He refused because it was Shabbos. They then told him to take a handkerchief with him, and he again refused. On the way to the Gestapo building the soldier asked my husband about his plans. This Gestapo agent, after hearing that we had paid for our trip to America, said to my husband, "The only thing that can save you is your belief in your religion, and I see that you have a strong belief. I will take you back. If you had not paid for your trip to America, not only would you be killed, but so would I." With the help of the Almighty, the trip had been paid and my husband was freed.

On January 17, 1939 we left Germany by airplane. It was the first time we had ever flown. We arrived in Rotterdam, Holland. From there we boarded a small ship to go to America. It was a pouring Friday afternoon when we arrived in America. Our cousin met us at the docks and took us to Washington Heights where we were to live for three months. We had finally come to these shores, thanks to the help of the Almighty, and to the wonderful people who were willing to give us an affidavit: my husband's brother, Reb Meir (Martin), who sacrificed his own affidavit for us; my niece Eva's first cousin, William Cohen, and our cousin Paul Herzog.

Reb Aharon Wehl with his brother Meir (Martin)

CHAPTER 2

A New Country

mi's tape continues as she relates the hope-filled, but difficult, early years in the United States. She and Opi would need all their strength of character to build a new life while maintaining the values that had nurtured them in Hamburg.

Our first Shabbos in America we stayed with a very nice family. Our thoughts, however, went back to our parents' homes, and to my father whom we had left behind. Suddenly tears came to my eyes. Then I realized that I was not alone. I had my husband and my child with me. At that time I said to my husband, "We must have courage. We want to begin building a new life, we cannot give up. The work may be hard but our thoughts are free."

We intended to give our son both a religious and a secular education. We were told that the best area to move to for this was Boro Park. There one could obtain both. We then looked for a small apartment. In those days apartments were already very expensive. However, we found a four-room apartment on a dead-end block, at 1727-54th Street. The rent was thirty-eight dollars per month. It was the cheapest we could find. We moved in with the furniture that we had brought from Europe. We lived on a very tight budget, even for those days. Four dollars and fifty cents covered our weekly expenses. On one occasion we reviewed our calculations a second time to look for the extra twenty-five cents that we had spent that week.

At that point in our lives we had to face a major issue, that of what to do to earn a living. It was impossible for my husband, who had been in real estate in Europe, to find a position in his field. My relatives and friends urged me to pursue my medical profession. They said, "Medicine is in your hands, you will be successful." It was a difficult choice for me. I agreed to undertake the task on one condition. I insisted that my young son, who was one and a half years old, should not be sent to a baby-sitter. He was to be cared for by my husband.

My first hurdle was to pass the "English Language" examination. In order to prepare for this test I went to a coaching school which was located on the Bowery. I had to be in class from seven to nine-thirty in the evening. My husband would pick me up from there. As you see he was always at my side, and even in the most difficult times he always encouraged me to continue further. While walking on the Bowery, I would often say to my husband, "I don't want to be able to buy anything for myself, but will I ever have a moment's time to do some window-shopping?" Those days were so rushed. The English examination was not easy. I failed it the first time. With additional coaching, I passed it the second time.

My major task now was to prepare for the State Board of Education Exam in Medicine. The year 1922, when I had taken my State Boards in Germany, had long since passed. It was 1940 now, and much of the theoretical aspects of anatomy and physiology were no longer fresh in my mind. In addition, the examination that was administered in Germany over a period of five months was given here in one day. It was a written examination. I failed it brilliantly. Six months later I tried to take it again, and this time I nearly passed. The only subjects that I did not pass were anatomy and physiology. I could not retake this part of the test for a whole year. The question then arose, what would we do during the coming year? We had to live. Some money had to start coming in to our household. I began working as a practical nurse. Nobody knew that I was a doctor. People did not like us, they called us 'the greener'. They thought that we were lazy and arrogant. I tried my best to prove to them that it wasn't true. At one home, I washed seventy-five diapers a day by hand since diaper service was not available then. My employer even dismissed her cleaning woman, since she had a 'greener' there to do all the work. My hands were bloody at times, but I never complained. Occasionally my husband brought me a candy bar that cost twenty-five cents and then I was the happiest person in the world.

Many of my nursing jobs were not in the neighborhood. Several of them were overnight positions. I not only washed the diapers in some homes, but also the clothing that belonged to other members of the family as well.

It was not easy. We could not afford a telephone in those days. Therefore, my husband had no way of knowing when I would come home. Once, on a Sunday, I traveled by train for two hours from the Bronx, only to arrive home and find that my husband and child were not there. They were visiting with family in Manhattan. I left a note on the table indicating that I had been there and returned to my job.

It may be difficult to believe, however, on many occasions during the ensuing years my mother referred to those times as the happiest days of her life.

It would be remiss of us in writing this book not to mention two families who in those difficult days became good friends of our parents. Both became involved with my mother at the time when she was doing practical nursing. Mr. and Mrs. Reuben Abzug, who hired my mother as a practical nurse after the birth of their son, became devoted friends of the Wehl family. Mr. and Mrs. Nordlicht, who owned one of the first *shomer Shabbos* (Sabbath-observant) grocery stores in Boro Park, provided the means of communication through which my mother was contacted. This was via the use of their telephone. The Nordlichts did not hesitate to walk the two avenue blocks from their store to the Wehl residence to relay messages.

In 1941 I received my medical license. At that time my little son shook his head and said, "My mommy got her license, now she will never go away." He didn't realize that my life would be hard and that he would not have it easy. He was a child of a professional mother, of an elderly couple, and of a family that had to make a new life in America.

We had to look for a different apartment. I felt that we should try to get one in a newly built apartment house. Young couples would move in there, and when they would have children perhaps they would use the doctor in the building. We moved into 1536-51st Street and I opened my first office in America. The apartment consisted of three-and-one-half rooms. One room was used as an examination room, the other as a waiting room, and the third as a bedroom. The kitchen was used by the patients to warm up their babies' bottles and their children's lunches. All our personal furniture was put into storage. In those years, I never slept on a bed, I only had a couch on which to rest.

In the 1943-1945 era, many male doctors were serving in the army, and so my office soon became crowded with patients. Earning a living at the beginning was a struggle. I still had to continue working as a practical nurse at night. In addition, I gave a course at the Red Cross. I also started to work in the Infants Home of Boro Park, a home for children without parents.

Life was hard then. Omi would tell us that at the time she started her office she had one good blouse that had cost her one dollar. This blouse was worn only when patients came to the office. A national Jewish organization was approached by Omi for help in starting her office. She was told, "You have three strikes against you: you are a woman, you are a foreigner, and you plan to observe the Shabbos. We cannot help you." After being turned down by this organization, Omi was helped by a two-hundred-dollar loan from Congregation B'nei Yehudah where Opi prayed regularly. Thus Omi started her office with two hundred dollars worth of assets, and with two hundred dollars worth of debts.

Many people could not understand that I did not have any office hours on Shabbos. "How will you make a living? Shabbos is the biggest business day in Boro Park." This was a question always asked of me in my beginning years as a doctor. Despite their arguments, I didn't have office hours on Shabbos, and with the help of the Almighty I was successful very soon.

In the beginning I did not have a car and I did not know how to drive one. After one year in practice, however, I realized the need for it. I had to make house calls that were not in the immediate neighborhood. During the summer I went out to visit my patients who had moved to the suburbs for their vacation. It took me a whole day to travel to Belle Harbor. In those days I would charge one dollar for an office visit, and two dollars for a house call. Thus, after traveling a whole day to and from Belle Harbor, I would come home tired and exhausted having earned nine dollars for the entire day.

The fees included much of the work that is done today by medical laboratories, including the taking and analyzing of the children's blood counts. Sometimes my husband and I would stay up to twelve or one o'clock at night recording the blood counts. Patients would bring dirty diapers for examination at any time, day or night. But despite all the difficulties, it was wonderful to be a doctor again. During the war years I was hired by the welfare group of Young Israel of Boro Park to be their doctor. The arrangement was that the members of this group would pay one dollar for an office visit and two dollars for a house call. After the war years were over, I felt that some of the members of this group did not require my services as a welfare doctor. The majority of these people remained with me as private patients. Included among them were two lay leaders of Boro Park Jewry, Jesse Deutsch and Henry Wechsler.

At this time I became acquainted with Mrs. Clara Wagner, a nurse at Maimonides Hospital who became one of our dearest friends. Among the nurses who worked with me during my years as a doctor, I am proud to mention: Mrs. Pearl Heschel Twersky, the daughter of the Kopitshnitzer Rebbe; Mrs. Eva Wasserman, the daughter-in-law of Reb Elchonon Wasserman (הי"ד); Mrs. Mira Lezer of the Meyer-Lezer family; Mrs. Ida Brown, and Mrs. Helen Dahlman who is my present nurse.

At this point in our lives we made an important decision. With much bitachon (trust in Hashem) we bought our house at 5015-15th Avenue. Little did we ever think that we, who "had three strikes against us," would, in such a short time, be able to purchase our own home. But the zechus avos (merit of our parents and of preceding generations), as well as the mesiras nefesh of shmiras Shabbos (selfless devotion to the observance of Shabbos) brought to us the siyata d'Shmaya (help from the Almighty) to obtain this home. On lag b'Omer of 5708 we celebrated with a chanukas habayis (housewarming). When I first saw the house I was skeptical. It was a very old house and it was in extremely poor condition. My husband, however, who was so well versed in real estate, told me not to worry. With painting, papering, and some renovation, he felt it could become a beautiful office. We made many alterations to the house. Besides creating a doctor's office in the front, we had to revise the living quarters in the back of the apartment. I still shudder when I think about the first time we saw the back bedroom of the house,

The
American Board of Pediatrics
hereby certifies that
Selma Wehl, M.D.
has successfully fulfilled the requirements of this board
as to competency to practice Pediatrics as a specialty
and is declared a
Licentiate of The American Board of Pediatrics

Attest: *Chas. J. McWilliam*
President.

Le Forest Hill
Secretary.

No. 3303

May 7, 1950

Selma Wehl, M.D., is certified as a member of The American Board of Pediatrics

with half a dozen chickens running around in it.

Although the practice was growing, I always felt that if one wished to benefit from the full rights that are given by a country, one must also be willing to accept full responsibility. This motivated me in 1950 to become a diplomate and fellow of the American Academy of Pediatrics. I applied to take the examination in that year. This test was divided into two parts, written and oral. I passed the American Specialty Board of Pediatrics examination. It was a special event to no longer be considered merely a European pediatrician. Now I was a full-fledged member of the American Academy of Pediatrics and had all the rights that belonged to an American pediatrician.

These rights were exercised many a time on behalf of the patient. Being an accredited pediatrician enabled Omi, who was a full-fledged staff member of the Maimonides Hospital of Boro Park, to have access to other hospitals as well. Thus she was able to visit patients, advise parents and consult with other doctors regarding her babies, while they were being taken care of in other hospitals.

The years rolled on. Yaakov finished his schooling and received

Rabbi Ephraim Zalman Halpern   Rabbi Yehudah Galinsky

smichah (ordination) from Yeshivah Rabbeinu Yaakov Yosef. He then brought us a new addition to our home, a wonderful girl, Hadassah. Our greatest pride was that she came from a home where both her father and grandfather spread Torah. Her parents, Rabbi Yehudah Dov zt"l and Rebbitzen Leah Galinsky, built a yeshivah in Coney Island. Her grandfather, Rabbi Ephraim Zalman Halpern, was the founder of the Merkas Leman Taharas Hamishpachah in Israel. The rosh hayeshivah, Rabbi Aharon Kotler, and his family, and Rabbi Wohlberg all spoke very highly of the Galinsky-Halpern family. We were very proud of the home the young couple built.

We saw that our own children were privileged to influence many students, among them, those who came from backgrounds that were non-Torah observant. They were instrumental in helping these youngsters become Bnei Torah (boys who continued learning Torah). We were thrilled and delighted to see that those values that we had learned in our parents' homes were being perpetuated in the home of the new generation. Our Purim seudah was frequently enhanced with the presence of some wonderful boys in Yaakov's class at the Hebrew Academy of Nassau County. The time of our marriage was a very turbulent period in Jewish history. In addition we were not youngsters. Our future was clouded with uncertainties. You can imagine the excitement and pride that we felt when twenty-five years after our arrival in America our first granddaughter was born. She was named after my husband's mother. In the meantime we have been blessed with additional grandchildren. They are all lovely, firmly rooted in Yiddishkeit and general knowledge. They show their love and devotion to us.

We had the opportunity of traveling quite a bit. We visited various sections of the United States and Canada. We had the zchus (privilege) of praying at kever avos (the graves of our parents) in Europe. We often toured Switzerland and its surroundings. The country that won our love and admiration was Israel. Just four years ago, my husband and I had the opportunity to once again (the fourth time) daven at the Kosel HaMaaravi (Western Wall). Despite the

Opi and Omi at the Kosel HaMaravi (summer of 1982)

fact that I had broken my hip on two separate occasions and required surgery I was able to enjoy those vacations. I am thankful to the Almighty for giving me the courage to continue my practice during the time of my infirmities. Whether it was from my hospital bed via use of the telephone or from the wheel chair on my return home, I was able to help my patients in need.

Our life was really a pleasant one, for which we have much to be thankful. Two years ago it suddenly changed. My husband was niftar very suddenly (within a period of twenty-four hours) on the 14th day of Iyar 5744 (May 16, 1984). He had a long life. Even on the last day of his life he managed to daven with talis and tefillin. As wonderful as my children and grandchildren are, life for me has become very lonely.

The tape has ended and yet we must mention that which Omi said on many occasions. Despite her loneliness she was thankful to the Almighty, not only for her grandchildren, but also for being privileged to see great-grandchildren as well. Several months after Opi was *niftar*, our daughter Chava married Zvi Weissman, from the distinguished Weissman family. Omi always remarked that history seemed to be repeating itself. Once again the family of Wehl had been joined together with an outstanding rabbinical family, that of Rabbi and Rebbetzin Simchah Weissman. Omi always felt that Opi would have loved Zvi for his wonderful *midos* which certainly complement his *Torah* and *avodah*. Zvi and Chava had two children during Omi's lifetime, a boy named after Opi and a baby girl. Omi spent much of her spare time knitting blankets and outfits for her great-grandchildren.

She took great pride in the closeness of the grandchildren to their grandparents. She used to boast about how wonderful it was to see the boys walking Opi to and from *shul* on Shabbos. Opi took great pride in his grandchildren, in their learning, in their *davening*, and in their exemplary *midos*. The boys *davened* with Opi in his *shul* and thus hopefully they will remember some of what they saw. The granddaughters spent many hours with Omi. They served as a source of consolation to her in these last years after Opi passed away. Omi was proud of the achievements of her grandchildren and particularly of the volunteer work the girls did in the areas of *bikur cholim* (visiting the Jewish Chronic Hospital almost daily) and shopping for people who were unable to leave their homes. She saw in them a fulfillment of what she had said in her *bar-mitzvah* message to her son. "We human beings don't appreciate what we have. We don't know how wonderful it is to see with our eyes and to hear with our ears. There are, unfortunately, people who are handicapped and who don't possess these precious gifts. It is there that I would like you to go and bring help and happiness. I know your time is limited, and that you spend most of the day in the *yeshivah*, but from time to time spend an evening in these homes." This message was instilled in her grandchildren.

CHAPTER 3

A Loyal Daughter

"When my father punished me, he would put me in the corner. It would have been better if he would have slapped me, for I never answered him back, even if I was devastated."

mi, from her youth on, always exhibited a great degree of *kibud av v'em* (respect for father and mother). This was manifested in many ways. Mrs. Sonya Bistritsky, a close friend of the family from Hamburg, came to visit during the *shivah** for Omi. She told us, "Neither you nor anybody in this room has really fulfilled the *mitzvah* of *kibud av v'em*. The only person I knew who performed it properly was your mother. When her parents would come to visit her at her medical office, she would set the table as if the Kaiser of Germany had come."

Omi, in her own tape, relates how when she rented a very elegant apartment in a new building in Hamburg for her medical office, she had one unused extra room. She said, "I told my mother, 'Let us go and buy beautiful furniture for the living room. Every Sunday afternoon, you and Dad have to come over and have cake and coffee with me in my apartment . . .' Every Sunday I rented a chauffeur-driven car to take my parents out and we had a wonderful time."

Once she came home and found her mother crying. It seems that a vast sum of money, ten thousand Dm (German currency), had been

---

*Shivah — week-long period of mourning observed by close family members after a death.

Rabbi and Mrs. Moshe Mordechai Lewin

lost. Her mother felt responsible for it and was extremely distressed. Omi thereupon said, "Mother, money is here today and gone tomorrow. Don't cry over money; I will never lack for it." She then replaced every single penny of it.

Omi would use the occasion of Purim to supply her parents with much of what they needed in foodstuff for a whole year. She would divide a table into four areas, with each area designated for another purpose. For example, one corner would have all kinds of canned goods on it.

Poem in honor of Opi and Omi's wedding

שִׁיר זֶמֶר לְיוֹם שִׂמְחַת לִבֵּנוּ

יוֹם א' כ"א אֲדָר תרצ"ו

נִגּוּן מָעוֹז צוּר

<u>אַהֲרֹן</u> הֶחָתָן גַּבַּאי נֶאֱמָן	הָבָה יְדִידִים נְזַמֵּרָה
עוֹסֵק בְּמִצְוֹת כָּל זְמָן	תְּהִלַּת ד' נְדַבֵּרָה
אוֹהֵב אֶת הַקָּלוֹם בְּלֵב וּבְנֶפֶשׁ	בְּחַסְדּוֹ לָנוּ מִצְוָה נָתַן
בְּלִי שֶׁמֶץ וְרֶפֶשׁ	לְשַׂמֵּחַ כַּלָּה וְחָתָן
עַתָּה הֵם מִתְיַחֲדִים	הָרְפֻאָה הַכַּלָּה <u>שָׂרָה</u>
לִהְיוֹת תָּמִיד אֲחָדִים	בְּאַהֲבָה עַזָּה שׁוֹמְרָה
לִבְנוֹת בַּיִת עַל יְסוֹד הַתּוֹרָה	הַיְלָדִים אֲשֶׁר הֵם חוֹלִים
וְלֵלֵךְ יַחְדָּיו בְּחִבָּה גְמוּרָה	וּמְצַפָּה לִישׁוּעָה מִמְּרוֹמִים
יְהִי ד' עִמָּכֶם	זֹאת תִּהְיֶה לָכֶם לְעֵזֶר
יְמַלֵּא מִשְׁאֲלוֹת לִבְּכֶם	וּלְכָל הַמִּשְׁפָּחָה לְגֵזֶר
הֱיוּ שָׂשִׂים וּשְׂמֵחִים	אֲשֶׁר תַּעֲלוּ לִקְדֻשָּׁה
כַּשָּׁעָה הַזֹּאת כָּל חַיֵּיכֶם	כַּאֲשֶׁר הָיְתָה לָנוּ יְרוּשָׁה

עִמְדוּ אֶת הַכּוֹסוֹת מַלְּאוּ
וְאֶת ד' הַטּוֹב הַלְּלוּ
שְׁתוּ לְשָׁלוֹם טוֹב וּלְחַיִּים
לְרֵעִים הָאֲהוּבִים הַשְּׁנַיִם

Another manifestation of this *kibud av v'em* took place on Rosh HaShanah and Yom Kippur. For many years Omi's father had a rabbinical position one-and-one-half-hours walking distance from home. Omi and her sister would rise at five o'clock in the morning on Rosh HaShanah in order to accompany their father to his *shul*. On Yom Kippur, when they did not want to leave their mother alone all day, they stayed with her until after *mussaf* (additional midday prayer). Then the sisters went on their lengthy trek in their special Yom Kippur shoes*, in order to hear the speech their father delivered before *neilah* (concluding prayer).

One might best summarize Omi's performance of this *mitzvah* in the words of her own father. As the acting Rav of Hamburg, he was the one who officiated at Omi and Opi's marriage ceremony. As is the German custom, he gave a speech during the marriage ceremony. He said: "And now my beloved daughter, without wanting to offend your sense of modesty, in the hour which is one of the happiest of my life, I must tell you, you always did bring sun, love and goodness into our house. Regardless of your successful striving and all the duties which your noble profession carries with it, and which you as a shining example of your profession fulfilled so loyally and conscientiously, you have never distanced yourself from your family, and you were happy and content only when you could show kindness and happiness to your parents, sister and brother ... You will establish and enrich your new home with the wealth of your knowledge, your abilities and know-how, and foremost with the fear of the Almighty which has distinguished you, not only since yesterday and today, but has been your inheritance from great ancestors and has always been a guiding beacon and a precious heirloom."

---

*On the fast day of Yom Kippur one is forbidden to wear shoes made of leather.

CHAPTER 4
The Man Behind the Scenes

" ... and to the memory of my dear husband who encouraged me in my work and helped me tremendously ... My husband was well known to my family because he came to a shiur (class) given by my father every Shabbos morning ... My mother therefore knew my husband, and was greatly in favor of him ... After my sister became engaged, I agreed to meet my husband."

ho was this wonderful husband who was to become her life partner in her sacred task of saving lives? Where did this person, who was willing to forfeit all his own personal conveniences, acquire such qualities? The inconveniences were innumerable! It entailed endless nights of sleeplessness; walking great distances on Shabbos in order to accompany the doctor to a patient's home; sitting alone on many a Shabbos and Yom Tov, because the doctor was desperately needed elsewhere, and just being there night and day to answer the telephone and bring assurance to an anxious caller. Opi tended all these charges *besever panim yafos* (with a pleasant and friendly disposition). Rabbi Gershon Weiss, the principal of the Yeshivah of Staten Island, who eulogized him, said he was the kind of person who typified the Jew that Rabbi Shamshon Raphael Hirsch had in mind when he spoke of *Torah im Derech Eretz*. [According to Rabbi Shamshon Raphael Hirsch's commentary on *Pirkei Avos* 2:2, "the term *derech eretz* is used primarily to refer to ways of earning a living, to the social order that

Opi, the man behind the scene

prevails on earth, as well as to the mores and considerations of
courtesy and propriety arising from social living and also to things
pertinent to good breeding and general education."] Where did these
qualities originate? From which sources did he receive the inspiration?

Reb Aharon Wehl, "Opi", was born in Hamburg, Germany, on the
5th day of Teves 5649 — Dec. 9th, 1888. Opi would always pride
himself with the fact that Hamburg was a member of the three
kehillos "AHW" — Altona-Hamburg-Wandsberg. They were
among the most distinguished communities of Orthodox Jewry in
Western Europe. He was proud of the fact that many *gedolei Torah*
and outstanding rabbis resided there, among them the renowned
Rabbi Yaakov Emden.

Those who knew Opi well, in America, saw in him the
perpetuation of those values. On the occasion of his ninetieth
birthday, he was presented with a *sefer* dealing with the lives of the

chachmei A-H-W. Rabbi Michal L. Munk, a close friend of the family, inscribed the sefer as follows:

Opi grew up in my grandfather's (Opa Wehl) house. Opa Wehl's home was a bastion of *Torah, avodah* and *gemillus chassadim* (Torah study, the service of G-d, and kind deeds). For many years Opa Wehl had his own *klaus* (small private shul). Not only was Opa Wehl responsible for the full operation of the *klaus*, he also had a learning group that met in his own home every Sunday morning. In fact, as our cousin Eva tells us, she recalls that whenever a *siyum* (festive meal upon completion of a tractate) took place in the house it was such a special occasion that the women even had to wear their "Shabbos aprons."

Opi would tell us that after *davening* on Friday night, Opa would always take those individuals who had not been invited elsewhere to his home for Shabbos. Once a neighbor who noticed that some of these guests wore shabby clothing asked: "Herr Wehl, how can you take these people home?" Without a moment's hesitation Opa Wehl answered, "Max Warburg (a very famous German millionaire) is not in need of my invitation."

Not only was the *mitzvah* of *hachnasas orchim* (hospitality) adhered to, it was fulfilled to the fullest extent. There were those guests who would not eat from the *schechitah* (ritually prepared meat) of Hamburg. They would always arrive on Wednesday when only a dairy meal was served. Some preferred to eat only rice cooked with milk and that was prepared for them. Some traveling Eastern European guests stayed from Succos to Succos. That was the kind of home it was.

Opi never really knew his mother. She passed away when he was four years old. Opi was the youngest of three brothers and two sisters. The burden of educating and bringing up Opi and his sisters and brothers fell upon their father (Opa Wehl) and the oldest sister Dora. His brothers made their mark. His older brother, Reb Meir (Martin), gave up his affidavit (a prerequisite to be admitted to America in those days) so that his brother Reb Aharon, his sister-in-law, and their son, Yaakov, could come and resettle on these shores. He felt that they could perpetuate the golden chain. Thus Reb Meir (may his memory be blessed) has a major share in this book and in all that has subsequently occurred since then. His second brother, Reb Nechemiah Yosef (Nehemias), became a very famous orthodox doctor. He headed the Rothschild Lung Sanatorium in Nordrach. His *mesiras nefesh* (self-sacrifice) in remaining with his patients prevented him from escaping the cruelties of the Nazi era. There are still people in America who, to this very day, cherish the letters they received from him. His sister Dora married the distinguished Reb Klonimus Englander, who unfortunately passed away at a very young age. They had two children, Carl who escaped to South Africa, and Eva who came to America and is very close to us until this very day.

Having been brought up in such a home, it was no wonder that while still very young, Opi developed a great measure of awe and reverence for a *shul* and for all that it represented. He always referred to the *shul*, as did our Sages, as a "*Mikdash me'at*" (a miniature Sanctuary). *Davening* in *shul* was as important to him, if not more so, than eating.

From the time that Opi was about thirteen years old he always stood during the complete *davening*. This practice which continued until he reached his middle eighties included the entire day of Yom Kippur. Once I asked Opi to explain the origin of this difficult custom to me. He told me that once, about the time he had become *bar-mitzvah*, he fell asleep in *shul* on Yom Kippur and from that day on he adopted this custom. In Hamburg, *shul* on Yom Kippur started at six a.m. and continued throughout the day without any recess! Yet, from then on, this young *bar-mitzvah* boy who had fallen asleep in *shul* on Yom Kippur took upon himself to stand without respite during *davening*.

Watching Opi *daven* was indeed an experience. He never moved. He stood as an *eved ha-omed lifnei haMelech*, a servant standing in front of the King. Those people who observed him praying frequently commented on the intensity of his concentration, despite the fact that barely a movement was visible. Talking in *shul* was out of the question. The desire to be in *shul* carried through to the very last days of his life. During the *shivah*, Reb Anshel Fink related the following incident: Mr. Wehl was well into his nineties when, one morning while passing Reb Anshel's house, he fell. Seeing what had happened, Reb Anshel immediately ran downstairs to see how he could help. Mr. Wehl had already risen from the sidewalk. At that point Mr. Wehl thanked Reb Anshel and insisted that he commit himself "not to tell anybody about this fall" for fear that if his wife or son would hear about it they might insist that he no longer leave for *shul* so early. Having no other choice, Reb Anshel agreed. It was only during *shivah* that he felt that he was free to tell the story.

Another episode occurred during a period when Opi had a problem with his eyesight. One morning Opi came to *shul* and found the doors locked. He then proceeded to return home and when he did he realized that the clock in the kitchen read three o'clock rather than five o'clock, the time he originally thought it was. When his son asked, "Opi, what did you do then?," he answered, "What do you mean, I went back to *shul* at five o'clock, of course!"

It was a sight to behold when Opi would leave the *shul*, because he always walked out of the *shul* backwards, much to the concern of those who observed him. That was the way he had done it in Hamburg and that was the way he did it on the next-to-last day of his life, as Rabbi Pollak eulogized him at the funeral.

Opi quoted, בבית אלקים נהלך ברגש, *We walk into the house of G-d when there is turmoil outside (Psalms* 55:15). The letters of ברגש, *turmoil*, form an acronym — ברד, *hail*; רוח, *wind*; גשם, *rain*; שלג, *snow*. Indeed in the *bar-mitzvah* speech to his son he said as follows: "No time can be too early in the morning, and no time too late in the evening, to go to the *beis medrash*," paraphrasing from the famous Talmudic text that we say every morning after reciting the *birchos haTorah* (blessings of the Torah). That text served as the basis of his whole address. At that moment he delivered the credo by which he lived by ending with the following statement: *"This world is only a vestibule for the coming world. Prepare yourself in this world so that you can enter the palace of the next world" (Pirkei Avos* 4:21).

His attendance at the *shiurim* was remarkable. His strength of commitment to a *shiur* led to a humorous incident at his own engagement. Opi, of course, had a *shiur* that night and even an engagement *seudah* couldn't waive that commitment. The *kallah* [Omi] had prepared a sumptuous meal, but the chocolate pudding was a total disaster. Instead of being a smooth pudding it was a lumpy concoction of milk and chocolate. However, when the dessert was finally served the chocolate pudding looked appetizing, as it should. Her father was very surprised but did not say a word. After the Wehl family had left the Lewin household, he asked her, "Selma, how did the lumpy pudding turn out so smooth and delectable?" She answered, "Mr. Wehl's *shiur* was so long and he arrived so late that I had enough time to prepare a whole new pudding."

Another such incident occurred when Opi's brother, Uncle Meir, had his fiftieth birthday. Aunt Dora's children Carl and Eva prepared a surprise party with all the trimmings, but they forgot that their two uncles had a *shiur* that night, so all their preparations were for naught.

This commitment to *shiurim* which started in his early youth during the Hamburg years continued in the *Chevra Shas* (study group in Talmud) of Congregation Shomrei Emunah of Boro Park led by Reb Dov Pekier. At a *kiddush* on Opi's ninetieth birthday Rabbi Emanuel Gottlieb, a leading member of the *Chevra Shas*, said: "It is remarkable to me that in all the years that Mr. Wehl was a member of the *Chevra Shas* his eyes never closed once during the learning session."

Not only did Opi admire and have the greatest respect for Torah, he also revered Torah scholars. In the years that he was in Hamburg, Germany, he had a regular class led by, as he would call him, a *saar haTorah* (prince and master of Torah), the *rosh yeshivah*, Rabbi S. Rabinow (who later became a member of the Moetzes Gedolah Hatorah of Agudath Yisrael in London). Once Rabbi Rabinow wanted to go back to Czechoslovakia to see his mother. The group that he was learning with approached each member to contribute

Opi studying Mishnayos in the armchair brought from Europe 48 years earlier

towards their *rosh yeshivah's* trip. Opi told them to return to him that night and that he would have his share waiting for them. Thereupon he went to the bank and removed the total cost of the trip from his bank account. When those doing the collecting returned he presented them with what he considered his share.

But it was not in *shul* alone that he made his mark. In his home, here in America, his grandchildren were privileged to see a man who almost never spoke idly but who sat and learned, whether it was *Tehillim, parshas hashavua, Ein Yaakov, Mishnayos* and above all, the *sefarim* of the Chofetz Chaim.

There was a time after a cataract operation when Opi found it difficult to attend the regular *Chevra Shas shiurim*. Omi spoke to Rabbi David Cohen, whose children were her patients, and who had deep admiration for Mr. and Dr. Wehl. She asked him to find a *chavrusa* (study partner) for Mr. Wehl. Rabbi David Cohen arranged for Rabbi Avrohom Gurewitz, a noted Torah scholar, to come to the house and learn with Opi. They learned *mesechta Zevachim*. Opi was so appreciative of his new *chavrusa* that, in his usual humble and reverent manner for *kavod hatorah*, he insisted on preparing a fresh urn of coffee and a plate of cookies for him each and every time he came.

His humility and an exceptional degree of tolerance radiated from him. Whether it was displayed to an apologetic patient who called in the middle of the night, perhaps necessitating his accompanying the doctor on a house call or to the hospital, or whether he waited up for her to return, or in *shul*, Opi proved his humility and self-effacement.

Opi's humility was also manifested in his unique custom after receiving an *aliyah* (call to the Torah). Opi sat at the end of a row in *shul* and when he would return to his seat after receiving an *aliyah*, he would remain standing at the beginning of the row until the people saw that he was there. During the *shivah* when I was retelling this virtue, a young man, Shmuel Shuss, suddenly interrupted and said, " You don't have to tell me this story, I was a participant in it. Once, when your father received an *aliyah*, I forgot his custom and continued learning my *Mishnah Brurah*. Finally, a gentleman from behind tapped me on my shoulder and said, 'Don't you realize Mr. Wehl is standing here?' Mr. Wehl, in his nineties, would not disturb someone in his twenties."

Children are the pride and joy of parents, and Opi certainly put a lot of strength into the upbringing of his son, Yaakov, who was named after Opi's father. The goal was to enable this new link in the Wehl chain to continue the wonderful heritage of previous generations, for this was the way that Opi, himself, had lived. This was so eloquently testified to by a beautiful letter dated February 16, 1939 that Opi received upon coming to New York. The letter, written by his *klaus* in Hamburg, apologized for the lack of a more formal farewell in honor of Opi's leaving Germany. Such a farewell was impossible at that time because of the Nazi era. The letter expresses the warm thanks of the members of the *alte und neue klaus* for all that Opi had done both as a member and as the leading officer of the *shul* ... "with utmost understanding and a continually open hand did you always work for the objectives and efforts of the *klaus* ... and in remembrance of your deceased father you kept this position as a worthy heir should ... " In fact at a dinner on Opi's ninety-fifth birthday held in his children's house, Opi said, "I see in the home of Yaakov and Hadassah the continuation of all those things that I saw in my father's house."

The extension of this chain was a seemingly insurmountable task. Coming to a new country with very few material resources, barely knowing the language, having to find a new job, were all hurdles that had to be overcome. But even in confronting these hurdles the main goal, that of the *chinuch* of his son, was foremost in his mind. Thus the older members of Congregation Bnei Yehudah still recall how father and three-year-old son came to *shul* every Shabbos, even in one of the worst blizzards. In fact when Opi took his first position here in America, in those lean years when Omi had just established herself, it was on the condition that Opi never start his workday before ten and never stay at the office later than three. Indeed, *hashgachah* (Divine guidance) provided him with that opportunity, by allowing him to join the firm of his old friend from Hamburg, Mr. Marcus Bistritsky. If you are wondering why Opi insisted on these bankers' hours, let me assure you that it was not to make life easier for himself, for Opi was up at five in the morning to go to *shul*, and was still up at twelve at night recording results of the blood counts that the doctor was analyzing through her microscope. So why then those bankers' hours? The reason was simply so that Opi could personally bring his son to and pick him up from *yeshivah* every single day. This association with the Bistritsky family lasted for many years until and beyond Mr. Bistritsky's passing.

Working with Mr. Bistritsky had certain fringe benefits. Among them was the preparation of coffee from coffee beans so that it should be *kosher* for Pesach. They used their own grinding machine. For all we know Opi may have been the first *mashgiach* of *kosher l'Pesach* coffee in modern times. Eminent rabbis used this homemade coffee for themselves.

He was always among the first customers to buy the *arba minim* (*lulav* and *esrog*), whether it was from Feldheim on the East Side or later from Reb Yechiel Niselbaum of Congregation Shomrei Emunah. Likewise, in the days when separate swimming facilities were unavailable, Opi would rise at six a.m. to go swimming together with a distinguished *mashgiach* of a world-renowned *yeshivah* at the Gordon Hotel in Hunter, New York. Observing Opi eating a *kzais* (prescribed amount) of whole unground *maror* (bitter herbs) on Pesach, one actually wondered how he could do it.

Yet his conduct was scrupulous not only *bein adam leMakom* (in his devotion to *mitzvos* between man and G-d) but also *bein adam lechavero* (in his behavior between man and his fellow man). For approximately thirty years he managed an apartment house in Boro Park. Due to the great shortage of apartments after World War II, many people would offer a financial incentive in order to obtain an apartment. He told us that never once did he take this *shlissel gelt* although it was offered to him innumerable times. Even when people offered this money for *tzedakah* (charity) he would tell them, "Tzedakah is something I do with my own money, nobody else's." Indeed, much of the money that Opi earned on his job was given away to charity. Maybe it was his honest way of giving *tzedakah* that merited him the privilege that the last check that he wrote in his lifetime was to Yeshivah Torah Vodaath. At the funeral Rabbi Shloma Yekusiel Bittersfeld, who resided in that apartment house for many years, eulogized him for his high level of truthfulness, integrity and *mentshlichkeit* (sensitivity and considerateness) in matters *bein adam lechavero*.

This same trait carried over into many other areas. Once when Opi, then over ninety years of age, came to comfort a mourner, one who had been friendly to him in *shul*, he found that the elevator in the building was not in operation. He proceeded to walk up all six flights of stairs in order to do this *mitzvah*. Needless to say the family was upset at that but Opi made nothing of it.

In referring to Opi's strong commitment to all these *midos* it would be remiss on our behalf not to mention the *shuls* in which he spent most of his time while he lived in Boro Park. One was Shomrei Emunah, originally under the leadership of Rabbi Wohlberg, who became a very close friend of the Wehl family through a life-saving episode with Dr. Wehl. Later the shul functioned, and still does, under the leadership of Rabbi Yaakov Pollak. Both of these eminent rabbis had an opportunity to evaluate and appreciate Reb Aharon for what he really was. Rabbi Pollak said many times: "Reb Aharon, although only a *Yisrael*, wore his *begadim* as Aharon the *Kohen Gadol* did, *l'kovod v'siferes*" (with honor and dignity).

In addition, there was a small German *minyan* (quorum of ten men gathered for prayer) organized in 1939 under the auspices of that wonderful individual, Rabbi Shemaya Wiesner. There, many of the customs and tunes of his younger years in Germany came alive again. It was there, at Wiesner's *minyan*, that Opi's *avodah* (prayer) on the *Yomim Noraim* (High Holy Days) was so obvious and carried so great an impact. Both a letter received after Opi's passing from Mr. Reiner Katzenstein as well as the eulogy that Dr. Meir Schick made at the *sheloshim* of Dr. Wehl made mention of the fact that they would never forget those days at Wiesner's, particularly how Opi stood throughout the entire *davening* and inspired those around him.

Opi, when asked after Yom Kippur how he felt, would sometimes in his later years say, "You know it isn't easy especially if one does not leave the *shul's* premises the whole day." In fact the end of every fast day was a moment of joy for him, not because he could now eat, but because the day *hat im gut farbygeshtanden*, he had been able to fast through the day. In all the years that I remember, I recall only once when he had to eat on Asarah B'Teves, under doctor's orders, because he was sick. I noticed that during the time he was eating he was crying and I remarked at the time to a *rosh yeshivah* that while it is possible for any ordinary person to fast, it takes an *ehrliche yid*

Opi had tremendous *hakaras hatov* (gratitude) for those people who made his goings and comings from *shul* easier. On Purim, one could see Opi running to personally deliver *shalach manos* to Reb Yosef Ash who, despite his morning rounds at the hospital as a leading member of the Bikur Cholim Society, found time to drive Opi home from *shul* in inclement weather.

Above and beyond much of what has been written so far, though, was Opi's loyalty, devotion and respect for his life partner. Who can count the hundreds and maybe thousands of times that Opi accompanied Omi on a house call? Whether it was on foot on Shabbos and Yom Tov, or whether it was in the car, Omi could always rely on Opi whenever she needed him. Citing particular instances almost takes away from the usual, yet we feel that some individual cases must be mentioned.

In the early years, after a *seder*, late at night, Opi accompanied Omi by foot to see a sick baby. The patient lived on Second Avenue, one and a half miles each way. They returned about two o'clock in the morning.

Their son, Yaakov, received a letter in camp describing how his parents had ended the fast on Tishah B'Av. Omi had to make a house call in New Jersey at seven o'clock in the evening to a patient whose family was spending the summer there. Of course, she was accompanied by Opi. Returning home, they pulled over to the side at the entrance to the Holland Tunnel and Opi got out of the car to *daven Maariv* (evening prayers). Then they each had a piece of cake, and a cup of coffee from a thermos bottle they had brought with them. That is one way of ending the fast.

While sitting *shivah* for Omi we found out that six years earlier Omi went to recheck a baby in the hospital at twelve-thirty at night. The mother, dumbstruck at seeing Dr. Wehl at that hour, couldn't understand why she was there and finally remarked, "Dr. Wehl, all alone at this hour of the night, isn't it dangerous?" Omi answered, "I am not alone, my husband is sitting outside in the car waiting for me." Opi was ninety-two years old at that time.

CHAPTER 5

A Shabbos Walk

"I came home at two o'clock in the night, my feet hurt me but I had the good feeling that I was not a mechalel Shabbos (a Sabbath desecrator)."

he sainted Chofetz Chaim, in a famous parable, compared the observance of Shabbos to the placard on the storefront of a business. When the sign is still intact, that is an indication that the business is still in operation; so too is Shabbos the true sign of every observant Jew. This applies to every single Jew. Some, though, are privileged to an even higher honor. Not only is Shabbos a sign and a symbol of their commitment to Orthodox Judaism, but by virtue of their observance, they themselves become a living symbol of its significance.

Omi was such a person. At a time when Boro Park was just beginning to flourish, almost all the stores remained open for business on Shabbos. A fully *shomer Shabbos* doctor was almost unheard of. It was during that time that Omi opened her office. Not only did she never have office hours on Shabbos, but she never drove the car to go to a patient on that day as well. This however did not prevent her from visiting and taking care of the infants and children who needed her attention. Her feet took the place of tires, just as her heart took the place of the motor.

Mr. Henry Wechsler related an incident that occurred about forty years ago. It was a Shabbos morning when the snowfall was of blizzard proportions. Not only were there no footprints visible, but one could not even see a dog in the street. Suddenly out of the

52 / HOUSE CALLS TO ETERNITY

desolation he noticed a small black figure in the distance. To his amazement, as this figure came closer he realized that it was none other than Dr. Wehl.

This episode was indicative of a lifetime pattern that continued well into her later years. Dr. and Mrs. Meir (Marvin) Schick tell of Dr. Wehl's devotion on a Shabbos in the spring of 1969. At this time Omi was seventy-two years old. "She had made a house call the day before but the next morning there was a knock on the door and there stood Dr. Wehl with her Shabbos bag. We will never forget the words she said to us as we stared at her in amazement. She said, 'My conscience just would not let me rest. I had to come and examine your daughter again.' " It still seems incredible that a doctor would make a house call on Shabbos on her own initiative just to be sure that her patient was properly diagnosed.

Her concern for a patient's welfare was not diminished by the restrictions imposed by the observance of Shabbos. We received this letter from West Palm Beach, Florida. "My son who is now forty years old had measles at the age of nine months. He was left with a very bad case of diarrhea. The doctor called me every morning and kept telling me to use different remedies. On Saturday she walked to my home (I lived on the fifth floor on forty-fifth street and twelfth avenue) and climbed up all the steps just to see how he was getting along."

Her black Shabbos bag, together with the stethoscope that was carried along with it, was a symbol of three major aspects of her life: her observance of Shabbos, her total devotion toward her patients, and her unstinting energy to do that which is correct without compromise. Thus many a time, the black bag was left at the patient's house to be returned after Shabbos.

Omi, in preparing her own tape, described one Shevuos day for us. It is true that every Shabbos and Yom Tov she was always on call, whether it was just before Opi was about to make *kiddush*, or in the middle of *kiddush*, or in the middle of the Shabbos meal. One might say that when the Day of Judgment comes, the cobblestones and concrete slabs of Boro Park will themselves testify to the echo of Omi's footsteps. Yet this particular Shevuos afternoon was slightly unusual. "First I walked to forty-ninth street and fifth avenue (a total distance of two-and-one-half miles). That evening I walked to Bay

Parkway and eighty-sixth street (two-and-one-half miles each way). I arrived home at two a.m. I had walked seven-and-one-half miles that day. My feet hurt me, but I had the good feeling that I had not desecrated Yom Tov."

A similar incident occurred on a Shabbos afternoon. Omi had just returned from making a house call on Ocean Parkway and Avenue M (one-and-three-quarter miles each way). It was pouring, and she came home soaked. The phone rang. I heard Omi say, "I was just at your sister's house across the street. I will be with you in a short while." Omi changed her wet clothes, drank a cup of coffee and was on her way again. A grand total of seven miles was walked in a period of three hours.

Simchas Torah is a very special day. Different communities celebrate it, each in their own manner. Twenty-one years ago, when she was almost seventy years old, Omi celebrated it this way. A baby who was born two weeks before suddenly developed a very high fever on the night of Simchas Torah. At 11:00 p.m. the baby seemed to be in distress. Omi was called. In order to avoid hospitalization, she remained at the patient's house until 4:00 a.m. As she left, she turned to the father of the child and said, "Mr. L., I expect to see you at my house before 7:00 a.m. to hear how the child is doing." This family has never forgotten that night. Never has Simchas Torah passed since then without some delicacy or flowers from that household on Omi's Yom Tov table. A week after the first Simchas Torah since Omi's demise, we received the following letter:

> Please accept this check to the Zichron Aharon and Frumet Sarah Wehl Fund. My mother used to send her flowers every Simchas Torah for *hakaros hatov* (appreciation) since she stayed up all night for me twenty-two years ago.
>
> May her memory be blessed,
> Aaron L.

During the forty-five years that Omi practiced medicine in the United States, it was rare for her not to walk to the hospital on Shabbos. In fact she often walked the three-quarter-mile distance each way two or three times on a Shabbos. A number of patients recalled some very touching incidents: A young woman related the following that occurred in 1978 when Omi was seventy-nine years old. "It was a Friday in January and I was fourteen. I left school early, doubled over with abdominal pain and went straight to Dr. Wehl's office. She examined me briefly, said it was probably appendicitis and sent me to a medical laboratory for a blood test. When the results supporting her diagnosis were received, she called Dr. Bertram Cohn (an eminent pediatric surgeon) and told him she was sending a patient to the hospital for an emergency appendectomy. As we left the office I vaguely heard her say, 'Don't worry. Everything will be all right . . . I'll be there when I can.' Surgery was scheduled for a little after 6:00 p.m., a short while after Shabbos had begun. I remember thinking what a great way this was to start a Shabbos. Then, as I was being strapped onto the operating table and hooked up to various monitors, I heard a familiar voice say, 'Hey, wait a minute. What are you doing? This goes over here, not over there.' Sure enough, there was Dr. Wehl in surgical dress. I was surprised to see her, since I really had not expected her to come. She came over to me, took my hand in hers and said, 'Don't worry, I'm here and I'm going to be sitting here during the surgery.' I thanked her for walking all the way to the hospital and apologized for disturbing her Shabbos, and being Dr. Wehl, she just patted my hand and said, 'Ach, please . . . of course I'm here. Everything is going to be just fine.' During the next week, not a day went by without a visit from Dr. Wehl to see how I was feeling. I truly feel privileged to have been her patient."

We all know the saying that one can make a mountain out of a molehill. As we perceived in the last incident, Omi had the knack of making a molehill out a mountain. Thus it is no wonder that a grandparent of a patient related the following tale. "After spending Friday night at the hospital with my sick grandchild, Dr. Wehl was about to go home. This was, of course, only after she was sure that the emergency room had all the correct instructions for aiding the baby. At the time when my grandchild began to breathe easier she prepared to leave the hospital and walk home. It was now 1:00 a.m. — in the middle of the night. The child's grandfather insisted on walking her, but it was only after much persuasion that she allowed him to."

This incident was repeated in a slightly different version on another occasion when Omi was already in her eighties. When she came home from the hospital at 1:00 a.m. on a Friday night, she found the baby's grandmother waiting for her at her home for a report on her grandchild's condition. She proceeded to lecture her about the dangers of walking the streets at that hour of the night. The woman lived two short city blocks away. Thus the doctor who literally walked hundreds of miles during the late evening and early morning hours of Shabbos expected this only of herself.

Many of Omi's colleagues wanted to relieve Omi of the burden of walking back home from the hospital. Often one of them would suggest to Omi that, as he was driving straight up fiftieth street, he would be happy to take her with him. To that she had a blunt response, "If you could drive me, then I could drive myself."

It was not purely for medical attention to an infant or a child that Omi would walk to the hospital on Shabbos. Wherever Omi felt that she could be a source of comfort or bring peace of mind to a patient, she would do so. An incident occurred twenty-five years ago that typified this approach. "One Friday night, while I was in the hospital recuperating from the birth of a stillborn child, who should walk in but Dr. Wehl. It was a freezing December night and in she walked. Before I could express my surprise, she stated matter-of-factly, 'I was out anyway seeing a sick child and the distance to the hospital was so short that I stepped in to make a Shabbos visit.' There was very little left for me to say after that. She gave me a lesson in life in the next few minutes. I had never experienced death before and I was feeling very sorry for myself. I could not accept the situation. By the time she left I was a different person. She had truly made a visit that is as well remembered and as much appreciated twenty-five years later as it was then."

There was another aspect of Shabbos that affected Omi's life. Dr. Meir Schick probably described it best of all at the eulogy delivered at the end of the thirty-day mourning period. "Dr. Wehl, I believe, had a category of patients whom we can call 'Shabbos patients.' These were people in the community who used other pediatricians. When a child became ill on Shabbos and their regular doctor was not available, there was 'Doctor Wehl just for Shabbos.' Just for Shabbos! Can you imagine? We know of the concept of a *Shabbos goy*. But that a doctor should exist for patients just for Shabbos, and obviously there was no remuneration! This service was not done because the patients were leaders of our community or special people, but rather just because she was Doctor Wehl, simply because she was so noble and so cognizant of her responsibilities as a doctor."

There was one occasion when Omi was faced with a major dilemma. This occurred during the influenza epidemic of 1947. At that time Omi turned to the great *gadol hador* (spiritual leader of the generation), Rabbi Aharon Kotler. She asked him how to tackle the problem of visiting so many patients, many of whom did not live in the immediate vicinity of her home, during the forthcoming Yom Tov of Succos. The *rosh yeshivah* decided that she should arrange to have a non-Jewish person drive her to see her patients. On that second day of Yom Tov, as we recall it, she made twenty-six house calls. This is what she said on the tape. "I gave the money away, not because I felt that I was so good, but because I wanted to make life hard for myself. I wanted to feel that these calls were a necessity. I did not want to feel that maybe on the following Shabbos there would be another *necessity* and that I might benefit from the money that I would earn." In retelling this incident to us, she used to say, "I am not so religious, I just wanted that the *heter* (permission granted) should not be taken too lightly, neither by myself nor by the patients." Thus every single patient had to either write out the check to a *yeshivah* or endorse it to one.

A most fitting conclusion to this chapter that deals with Omi's sacrifices on behalf of Shabbos is an episode that occurred after her death. At her burial, it was announced that no one should touch her *aron* (casket), or be involved with covering the *aron* and digging the grave unless he was a *shomer Shabbos* (Sabbath observer). Six weeks later, a young man came and told me that he was so moved by what he heard and saw at the funeral, that from that day on he became a full *shomer Shabbos* and was learning *mishnayos* every single day. Thus, even in death Omi was able to promote *shemiras Shabbos*.

CHAPTER 6

A Different Way
of Celebrating Yom Tov

"Look at these chairs ... I washed them with my own hands."

esach is a special time of the year for everybody. In fact one might say that Pesach begins as Purim ends for in most religious homes, once the Purim *seudah* is over, one begins to think of cleaning the house and getting it ready for Pesach. In Omi's home this was no simple task. 'Seeing is believing' is an expression that would apply to the tremendous volume of *shalach manos* that graced Omi's living room, dining room, kitchen and office. Purim was a day when many patients could show some form of appreciation for all that Omi had done for them. Omi valued their thoughtfulness. It is hard to imagine a house laden with fifteen pineapples, fifty bottles of wine and liquor, homemade *challahs*, pounds and pounds of cake and dozens of boxes of candy. Much of the *shalach manos* was given to a *yeshivah* where the students had a mini-*seudah* in honor of Shushan Purim. Omi would always tell us that her mother, who as a Rabbi's wife had received a lot of *shalach manos*, would say, "It's a pity that Pesach is so close to Purim."

Pesach was a very busy season for Omi. Not only did she have to conduct her office, home and hospital visitations as usual, she was also burdened with answering many questions regarding the permissibility of various medications on Pesach. Of course, Omi would always tell the patients, "Now that you have all the information, you must go and ask your rabbi. I am only a doctor; I am not a rabbi." Once a close student of Rabbi Yaakov Kamenetzky, after discussing a problem relating to Pesach with Omi, went to confirm the doctor's view with the late *rosh yeshivah*. Thereupon, Rabbi Yaakov Kamenetzky said, "You may do exactly as she said. I really wonder if the community of Boro Park realizes what an outstanding person it has in its midst in Dr. Wehl."

Despite all this, Omi took a personal hand in even the minutest details of the preparations. The day after Purim, the cleanup for Pesach began. Omi and Opi would be directly involved in the Pesach preparations. Despite their advanced age, they climbed stepstools, cleaned out drawers and went shopping for the Pesach food. Mrs. Halpern, a dear and devoted patient, related the following anecdote. It was *erev Pesach* and Omi took Mrs. Halpern into her dining room and said to her, "Look at these chairs which we use the whole year; I washed them with my own hands. I never let the cleaning lady do things for Pesach without my personal supervision. Look how beautiful they look." Omi continued, "I awoke this morning before six o'clock to cook for Yom Tov. After all, later on, I must be ready for my patients."

Omi's commitment to the observance of the laws of Pesach was phenomenal. For approximately twenty-five years, the second-floor apartment in her house was left vacant solely for the purpose of having a separate Pesach apartment. The main part of this apartment was its fully equipped kitchen. It is hard to visualize how many times Omi would run up and down the stairs, in between seeing patients, to check the meat on the stove, or the cake in the oven. Omi's nut cake was something that many of her friends enjoyed. This cake was topped with her personally made lemon cream. In the last four years of Omi's life, after we had moved into the house with our parents, the second floor became our apartment. This in no way diminished her zeal for a separate Pesach apartment. Many of her patients and her friends were shown her new Pesach apartment in another part of the house.

Omi was so stringent not only in her personal life. Weeks in advance of Pesach, she would prepare the patients for the upcoming Yom Tov. In planning the formulas and food diets for the infants, she could be heard repeatedly saying, "I am giving you this food for the baby now, for in two months Pesach will be here and by then the baby will be accustomed to the food."

A young lady graduating from Bais Yaakov of Boro Park attested to this in a letter handed to us after Omi's *petirah*. In the letter she writes, "Dr. Wehl was not only a doctor. Just last week (the week of the *petirah*), my mother was at the office. Dr. Wehl reminded my mother to get the baby accustomed to 'Pesach cereal.' Her strict adherence to the observance of *mitzvos* was unbelievable. "This is the impression that remained with a young teenager.

All this did not detract from her tremendous sense of responsibility towards her patients. Not only did Yom Tov mean seeing her own patients, but as already mentioned, Omi had a category of 'Shabbos and Yom Tov patients.' Rabbi David Grossman, the director of the Bikur Cholim Society of Boro Park, told us that he customarily goes to the *mikveh* (ritualarium) on Friday in preparation for Shabbos. This is a custom followed by many Jews. While at the *mikveh* he mentioned that Dr. Wehl had passed away, and he began describing the terrible loss it was for the community. At this point, a gentleman who was there spoke up and said, "You don't have to tell me about Dr. Wehl's deeds. We were not patients of Dr. Wehl. It was *erev Pesach*. Suddenly my child became ill. We could not reach our regular doctor; he was away for the holidays. Someone suggested that we call Dr. Wehl. Despite feeling awkward about doing that, we had no alternative. We called her and she came to our house. It seemed that the baby was having an outbreak of hives as a result of some kind of allergic reaction. Dr. Wehl called the pharmacy, waited for the delivery of the medicine, made sure that we gave the correct dosage, and remained in our home until the medicine took effect. We were not patients of Dr. Wehl, and we did not become patients of Dr. Wehl. This was a pure act of *chesed*."

The *seder* night of Pesach is the climax of all the work and effort which precedes it. The attention of all is focused on the *Hagaddah* and the *mitzvos* of the evening. The only time that one thinks of the 'door' is after *birchas hamazon* (grace after the meal), when the door is opened up for Eliyahu the prophet. In our home attention was always paid to the door. Rarely did a *seder* take place when there wasn't a slightly timid knock at the door with someone apologetically waiting there. Whether it was Omi's own patient or an out-of-town visitor in Boro Park for Yom Tov seeking advice, each received a full and complete response. Much of the time this response included a pause in our *seder* as Omi left to make a house call. One *seder* night we accompanied Omi on a call to the home of the B. family, who lived four flights up. On the way home from the call, a dog darted out from a dark alley and bit Omi on the leg. This required a further interruption in our *seder*, as we had to trace the ownership of the dog to avoid the necessity of taking rabies shots. There is an interesting sidelight to this story that reflects upon Omi's strength of character. This incident occurred about twenty-five years ago. This past summer, while we were *menachem avel* that family, the mourners were recalling how Omi interrupted her *seder* to visit their sick child. We mentioned the incident involving the dog; they were stunned. They had never been told about it. Obviously Omi didn't find it important enough to mention to them.

❀ ❀ ❀

In many homes it is customary that the men remain awake Shevuos night to study Torah. They either go to their local *shul* or learn in their homes. But it is rare that the women of the house remain up as well. Our home was different. Mrs. Devorah Schechter, a dear and devoted patient of Dr. Wehl, tells: "It was a Shevuos night when one of our children developed a croupy cough. Dr. Wehl was roused from her bed. She never complained when she was awakened at night; rather, she always gave us advice. In this particular case, she made a house call. The results of her examination convinced her that the child needed medication. It was three o'clock in the morning. Dr. Wehl and I walked to our local drugstore. The pharmacist who lived on top of his drug store, hearing the noises from outside, stuck his head out the window. He could not imagine who was disturbing his sleep. Dr. Wehl convinced him to get up, get dressed, come down, open the pharmacy and dispense the necessary medication. He was not very excited about the whole project, but she really did not care what he thought. She knew that the medicine was needed and that was the end of it. When Omi got home, Opi had finished saying *tikun leil Shevuos* (special learning program), and they both enjoyed a fresh cup of coffee. A truly unique way to celebrate the night of Shevuos."

❀ ❀ ❀

Every Yom Tov has its own distinctive *mitzvah*. One of the first additions to our house was a porch in the backyard. This enabled us to build a *sukkah* that was an extension of our house. We could walk straight out from our dining room into the *sukkah*. This *sukkah* was not used exclusively by our family. Our neighbors and friends who did not have a *sukkah* were most welcome. Opi and Omi's hospitality extended beyond that. Whenever Omi saw a religious intern at Maimonides Hospital, she would invite him to eat all his meals in our *sukkah*. He was made to feel at home, even to the extent of giving him a key to the house, so he would be free to enter and leave as he pleased. On one such occasion, this *mitzvah* helped us in an unforgettable manner. We had a steam pipe in our kitchen. As boys usually do, I leaned back with my chair against the pipe. The next thing I was aware of was the face of Dr. Chaim Sahtz looking down at me. I obviously had fallen back, hit my head against the pipe and suffered a temporary blackout. At that time Dr. Sahtz was coming to eat his lunch in the *sukkah*. Thus, the fulfillment of the *mitzvah* of *sukkah* may have been a much greater favor to me than to Dr. Sahtz.

Rabbi Chaim Boruch Wechsler, the son of Mr. and Mrs. Joseph Wechsler, dear friends of Omi's, always volunteered to blow the *shofar* (ram's horn sounded on High Holy Days) and read the *Megillah* (Scroll of Esther) for Omi in her later years. Rabbi Wechsler would go out of his way to try to come to Omi's house early, for he knew that Omi would not eat before hearing the *shofar*.

CHAPTER 7

The Mitzvah of the Eighth Day

"They are going to be taking another bilirubin test in the afternoon. I told them to let me know the results by three-thirty, but don't worry, I will call them. It is a short day, but I know you can still make the bris until four-thirty."

he *mitzvah* of *bris milah* (circumcision) on the eighth day is so significant that it has to be performed on Shabbos and on Yom Kippur (unless the baby was born through Caesarean section). Omi's devotion to that commandment was astounding. Dozens of phone calls, hospital visits, and consultations with *mohelim* (one who performs the circumcision) would be made in order to insure that the *mitzvah* be performed on the prescribed day. Omi at times would even admonish patients by telling them, "It is not so important that your whole family be present at the circumcision; if they can't get home from work in time, then the *bris* will have to take place without them, but it must take place on the eighth day." Thus, Omi would almost hound the local medical laboratories to conduct continuous testing of the infant's blood when the bilirubin count, which is indicative of the degree of jaundice in the baby, was high.

An out-of-town patient related: "We will always remember Dr. Wehl for her unique blend of kindness, superb medical knowledge, and *shmiras hamitzvos* (observance of the laws). I had the opportunity to witness this combination one Friday afternoon when Dr. Wehl graciously agreed to see a sick child of ours while we were visiting in Boro Park from out-of-town. The examination was briefly interrupted by the ringing of the phone, a short conversation, and a caller being put on hold. Dr. Wehl then called the medical laboratory, after which she returned to the caller on the other line, telling her, "Yes, you can have the *bris* tomorrow, *gezunterheit*."

Not only telephone calls were made to insure the performance of the *mitzvah*. Two of the outstanding *mohelim* in Boro Park, Rabbi Moshe B. Pirutinsky and Rabbi Yosef Goldberg, attest to her strong determination and physical sacrifice to insure that a *bris* would take place at the proper time. Rabbi Pirutinsky personally recalls the many times that he met Omi at the hospital on Shabbos, rechecking a baby to see if the infant was medically fit for the *bris* to take place. As Rabbi Pirutinsky said to us, "It wasn't easy for her to walk back and forth in all kinds of weather just to check if the yellow (jaundice) had receded."

Frequently a *mohel* who had doubts about the health of a child would only circumcise that child if Omi was willing to assume the responsibility. Rabbi Goldberg related the following incident during the *shivah:* "An infant was born in Maimonides Hospital in Brooklyn, to parents who resided in Queens. After seeing the baby I felt that I could not circumcise the child unless Dr. Wehl would assume full responsibility. This she did. Not only was she present at the *bris*, but the next day, after the family returned to Queens, she traveled out to see the baby. This was her concept of responsibility. In addition, she showed me what a remarkable person she really was. She came to my home in the morning to pick me up and said, 'Rabbi Goldberg, why should you make that difficult trip to Queens by subway to change the bandage? I will drive you there.' "

Omi's expertise and devotion in this area can best be summarized by an incident that occurred involving the distinguished *rosh yeshivah*, Rabbi Yitzchak Hutner. A close *talmid* of his, Rabbi Pinchas Kahn, who himself is a *rosh yeshivah* today, related the following incident. Once in his student years, a young married friend of his was unsure as to whether his son's *bris milah* could be on time. The friend asked Rabbi Kahn to discuss it with Rabbi Hutner, who mentioned that there was one *mohel* and one doctor medically equipped to solve this problem. "That doctor was Dr. Wehl. The *rosh yeshivah* was very surprised that I had never heard of her." Rabbi Hutner's advice was, 'Check out the problem with Dr. Wehl and whatever she says you can rely on.' "

Today there are hundreds of members of *klal Yisrael* (the Jewish people) whose circumcisions occurred on the eighth day, thus entering *bris shel Avraham Aveinu b'eto u'bizmano** (covenant of our Patriarch Avraham at the precise time), due only to the uncompromising principles and untiring efforts of Omi.

**This is the customary blessing given to a newborn male and his parents upon the father's being called up to the Torah after the child's birth.*

CHAPTER 8

In Appreciation

"He did me a favor when I came to America. I will never forget it."

One of the basic attributes of the Torah is *hakaras hatov* (the recognition of good). It is not by chance that we are taught in the Torah that Moshe *Rabbeinu* could not personally execute some of the ten plagues, such as turning water into blood. That would have constituted a lack of the proper degree of gratitude, a lack of recognition of the fact that it was water that enabled Moshe to survive in his little bassinet and temporarily escape the clutches of Pharaoh's wicked servants. Thus even such a great mandate as the emancipation of the Jewish nation from the land of Egypt and universal declaration of Hashem's sovereignty could not supersede the concept of *hakaras hatov*.

Omi appreciated any kind deed that was done for her. Years after the fact, she would recall how certain people had helped her become established in America. Thus, when she read that someone who had helped her forty years before had passed away, she immediately tried to find out how she could contact the family to comfort them at the time of their loss.

During the *shivah* a very well-to-do and prominent businessman related the following incident to us. His family only used Dr. Wehl when their cousin, who was a pediatrician, went away on vacation, and Omi never charged them for her services. The philanthropist was very upset since he could well afford to pay and since, as a matter of principle, it disturbed him to feel that he was taking advantage of

Omi. Finally he decided that he would try to convince her to accept her regular fee from him. Under much pressure Omi finally told him, "You are making a mistake, Mr. X. I am extending you a courtesy only because you are related to this pediatrician. He did me a favor when I came to America. I will never forget it; and therefore I am not charging you." Thus, Omi, forty years after coming to America, recalled the favor that someone had done for her.

At the time of Opi's cataract operation he had to remain in the house for a number of Shabbosim. Opi was extremely disturbed that he could not hear the reading of the weekly portion of the Torah. Likewise he could not review the portion of the week as he customarily did. One of Omi's long-standing patients suggested that her son would be willing to come and read the *parshah* for Opi on Shabbos, which the young man did. Omi never forgot this kindness. Despite the fact that during those years of the doctor-patient relationship with this family Omi had spent at least a dozen long nights at their home caring for the children, she constantly reminded the young man of the favor he had done. Even years later when this same young man married, had his own family, and used Omi as the pediatrician for his children, he told us, "Every time I came into the office, your mother always reminded me of what I had done so many years ago. She never let me forget it."

This sensitivity to *hakaras hatov* resulted in the development of a truly intimate and reciprocal relationship between Omi and her family on the one hand, and the household of the great Rabbi Aharon Kotler on the other. Omi had the greatest reverence for them and she was willing to do whatever was in her power, day or night, to be at their beck and call. Omi used to say that the Rebbetzin was the wisest and most wonderful woman she had ever met. On the other hand, the *hakaras hatov* the *rosh yeshivah's* family felt for Omi was remarkable. Thus it was possible for me, even at a young age, to develop a strong relationship with the *rosh yeshivah*. On numerous occasions I, myself, was privileged to drive Rabbi Kotler to several important appointments. I recall specifically one such occasion. The *rosh yeshivah* was engrossed in his learning of the *Mishnah Brurah* in the front seat of my car. Two young men, who were sitting in the back of the car, were discussing the recent illness of one of them, a very busy and prominent community worker. The latter remarked to his friend that, as a result of his illness, he finally had time to catch up with his reading the New York Times. The *rosh yeshivah*, who was seemingly involved in his learning, suddenly said, "Reb —— if you don't have a *gemara* in your home, I would be most happy to lend you one."

Another incident which also bears relating occurred after Rabbi Kotler had become ill. A special separate apartment was provided for him on the sixth floor of the building in which he lived, in order to try to stem the flow of visitors who would come to see him at all hours of the day and night. One Friday night, after we had finished our *Shabbos* meal I went up to say *gut Shabbos* (traditional Sabbath greeting) to the *rosh yeshivah* The Rebbetzin had almost finished serving supper and she asked the *rosh yeshivah* if he would like some fruit. He answered in the negative. At that point she said, "But Reb Yaakov's parents sent us a basket of fruit." Whereupon the reply was, "Yes, I would like an apple." After making the blessing and eating a piece of the apple, he turned to me and said, "Go home and tell your parents that the fruit tasted very good." Not only did the *rosh yeshivah* perform the marriage ceremony at our wedding, but the family also presented us with a *kiddush* cup and *sefarim* which are

At Yaakov and Hadassah Wehl's wedding — seated at the head table are (left to right) Rabbi Hersh Ginsburg, שליט"א; Rabbi Yitzchak Tendler, זצ"ל; Rabbi Mendel Kravitz, שליט"א; the chosson; Opi זצ"ל; Rabbi Aharon Kotler, זצ"ל; the Kapitshnitzer Rebbe, זצ"ל; and Rabbi Eliezer Karp, שליט"א.

being used to this very day. This connection was not terminated with the *petirah* of the *rosh yeshivah*. His son and great successor, Rabbi Schneur Kotler, and his Rebbitzen, despite their hectic schedules, found time on *erev Rosh HaShanah* to call Omi personally and wish her a good year. We are indeed fortunate to have become attached to the tree of life that holds *klal Yisrael* together.

Hakaras hatov by its very nature is a process that involves two parties and two situations. By definition, reciprocating 'for the good that was done' implies that there is a recognition by one of the parties that some good was done to them. In the many years of Omi's practice she was usually at the giving end, using all her physical and mental capacities to help others. During the last two or three years of her life, after Opi had already passed away, Shabbos sometimes appeared to be a long and lonely day. Despite the fact that she was surrounded by her children and grandchildren, things were not the same. Thus some of the people who had benefited from Omi's relationship with them over the years had the chance to reciprocate for the kindness she had shown to them. In addition to our Aunt Irma, Omi's sister, who would at times spend Shabbos with her, there were some friends who would visit Omi from Shabbos to Shabbos to keep her company. It would be remiss of us, knowing Omi's strong feeling of gratitude, not to mention Reb. Martha Munk, Mrs. Rose Stern, Mrs. Lillian Wechsler, Reb. Gisele Horowitz and Reb. Regina Bittersfeld, all of whom shared in making Omi's Shabbosim a little more pleasant.

Omi always was proud of a letter that she had received when her son Yaakov was born. The writer wrote, "If just a little of all the good that you have done to others would find its way back to you and your family, then your family will always be blessed." The family hopes that it will merit this blessing.

CHAPTER 9

Why Pediatrics

" ... *Then I got my training in the University Hospital. I enjoyed it tremendously. I started to work in the Public Health Station. At that point I had to make a decision as to which field of medicine I would choose. I chose pediatrics. Why? ... I saw in pediatrics the development of a new life — from the infant who, when he is brought into the office the first time, is not even able to move his head yet, to the confident teenager almost ready to handle his world. Slowly the child progresses from stage to stage. As the infant develops, he starts to cry on the examination table, realizing he is in a different environment. With the passing of time, he is sitting up, standing up, smiling, laughing at his parents, and crying at strangers, a living proof of the great miracle of the Almighty's creation. If you would ask me today if I would choose pediatrics again, I would answer, 'Yes'.*"

mi's love for, and devotion to, the field of pediatrics was based on her profound recognition of the value of life. She deeply appreciated this exceptional gift that the Almighty has given us. Her sense of fulfillment was best achieved through a synthesis of appreciation of her own lot, while simultaneously working to help her fellow man. That feeling of sharing in the happiness of others reached its fruition when a patient would tell her that she was expecting another child. She lived both through the anxieties and the anticipated joys, together with the patient. A mother who, unfortunately, had lost two children was advised by doctors not to have any other children. This woman called us after the *shivah* and said, "Do you know why I have six children today? It is all due to your mother's encouragement. While every other doctor stressed the negative, she persuaded us not to listen. With the help of the Almighty, despite our tragic losses, today we have a beautiful family."

Scroll presented to Dr. Wehl by the medical staff of Maimonides Medical Center

MEDICAL STAFF
OF THE
MAIMONIDES
MEDICAL CENTER

This Scroll is presented to

Selma Wehl, M.D.

In appreciation of the many years of distinguished service to the hospital and the community whose welfare it serves.

Your unselfish efforts on behalf of the institution and your unfailing concern for the sick have won for you the affection and respect of all who know you.

MAY 1, 1983

Jacob Solome, M.D.
President, Medical Staff

Omi's ability to participate in someone else's joy was so immense that at times it transcended any other emotional feelings she may have had. A patient told us of a remarkable incident that occurred during the week that we sat *shivah* for Opi. "Dr. Wehl was like a mother to me. I never hesitated to call her and she was always there when needed. She not only cared for her patients medically but also emotionally. I, myself, was her patient and so was my mother. I did not have children for some time after I was married. Dr. Wehl always inquired about my welfare when my mother came to visit her. She always told her, 'Tell your daughter not to worry. She will have children.' She always offered me words of encouragement. When my mother went to comfort Dr. Wehl when she was sitting *shivah* for her husband, she, as usual, asked about me. When my mother told her that I was expecting a baby, my mother said that she had never seen Dr. Wehl become so excited as at that time, even though it was a time of grief for her."

At times Omi's expression of joy manifested itself in a totally different manner. She enjoyed knitting for her grandchildren and great-grandchildren. It became a major hobby for her in her later years. Many nights after the last patient had left the office, Omi would go back to her knitting. Her greatest pride was when one of her grandchildren would come to visit her wearing a sweater that Omi herself had made. Every one of the grandchildren and great-grandchildren is the proud possessor of a hand-knitted blanket that Omi made. But it was not only for them that this was done. When someone who had had a prior tragedy, or who had not had any children for many years, informed Omi that she was expecting a baby, Omi would sometimes knit a blanket for the upcoming *simchah* (joyous event). She spent hours doing tedious work just to share in someone else's joy. The ability to devote so much time to this work was really the result of a feeling that the happy occasion was not only the patient's, but also partially hers too. This trait was described by a dear patient and friend. "Her commitments to her patients were the commitments of a mother to her child. For after all, our children were her children too. She shared in our joys, and she suffered in our grief. She agonized together with us as we endured crises. The relief in her voice when a child recovered from a critical illness cannot be compared with the cool tones of an indifferent practitioner of medicine waiting to collect a fee. No, hers was the voice of a dear relative who suffered along with us. Multiply this suffering by the thousands of children she treated, and one begins to realize the selflessness of Dr. Wehl."

Omi practiced medicine for sixty years and she saw countless numbers of children. Her love for each child was unique and she viewed every child as a special individual. This was movingly expressed by Rabbi Gershon Weiss when he said, "She was a messenger of Hashem to bring goodness to our children. At the same time we learned an enormous amount from her. I usually had the privilege of bringing my children to the office and I enjoyed my visit there. I enjoyed talking to her and watching the respect that she showed to others. When she examined a baby it was with love. The baby wasn't just an object. Even though she had seen thousands and thousands of babies, she loved each particular baby. When the doctor would put her fingers into the hand of a little baby and say, 'It has a good grip,' one saw her true love for that baby and the pleasure she took in its achievement."

This love for and dedication to each individual child was felt by the children themselves. Thus it was not surprising that various children thought of Omi during the summers they spent in camps or on trips. These same children found it necessary to express their feelings in letters which they sent to us during the weeks following Omi's *petirah* just as they had made *Rofeh Chol Basar* signs or brought home trinkets for her during her lifetime.

❦ ❦ ❦

"I have a funeral today." "Who?" — "Dr. . . . " (Mother could not finish the words). I said, "Wehl?" The response was a nod. My eyes filled with tears, I couldn't breathe, I was shocked. "I can't believe it," I stuttered. In those few minutes I relived in my mind everything I knew of Dr. Wehl in the four years that I had known her . . . She will always remain in my memory. Words cannot suffice to tell who she was. She was too great to describe. We lost more than a doctor. We all lost a friend and helper.

❦ ❦ ❦

At a *siyum mishnayos*, a little five-year-old boy was quoted as saying, "I hope *Moshiach* (Messiah) comes soon so that I will see my zeide and Dr. Wehl."

❧ ❧ ❧

Dear Family Wehl, " . . . I am very sorry to hear about the sudden death of the dedicated, honorable Dr. Wehl. I am only ten-and-one-half-years old. But for all it is worth I owe my life to Dr. Wehl, the messenger that Hashem sent me ten-and-one-half years ago . . . She became my pediatrician soon after I was born. She was always there for me. She was wonderful. Today I am B.H. fine and healthy. I am grateful to the Almighty for sending Dr. Wehl to me. She was the most dedicated and sincere doctor I have ever met. She will be missed by many. She was a special woman who surely deserves her place in *Gan Eden*. Dr. Wehl will always be alive in my heart. Her goodness and her help will be remembered forever."

❧ ❧ ❧

This beautiful poem was written by a young lady, Miss Miriam Guttman:

In Memory of Doctor Wehl

It was a shock, a sudden surprise
Tears of sadness sprang to my eyes
The news of Dr. Wehl's untimely passing filled me with disbelief
As I felt an overwhelming sense of loss and grief
She was a doctor who was adored
No patient's needs were ever ignored
Their welfare was uppermost in her mind
She was extremely devoted and kind
Her wonderful character made her shine
Revealing a person who was gentle and fine
Her modesty manifested itself in many ways
She always disliked hearing a well-deserved praise
Whenever a child walked into her office not feeling well
The look of concern on her face one was able to tell
She was always available from morning through night
To help a patient who was in a desperate plight
A devoted doctor like Doctor Wehl is very rare
She treated her patients with unlimited amount of loving care

Images of her will always flash in my mind
Pictures of a doctor who was caring and kind.

❦   ❦   ❦

A distinguished and prominent educator, Rabbi Yehudah Oel-baum, wrote, "Your mother comforted others even at times when she had to find comfort for her own situation. She had the special privilege of being a mother in Israel to several generations of *b'nei Yisrael*, and left an indelible impression on everyone who met her."

CHAPTER 10

Medicine at Her Fingertips

"In preparing for the qualifying examination for univer-sity, I realized that I had missed many things that others learned in college. I wanted to be finished quickly. I wanted to accomplish in six months what others completed during their entire college career."

rom Omi's beginning years in the field of medicine until her very last day, she was blessed by the Almighty with a phenomenal mind. Not only was she able to prepare for her matriculation examination in six months, but as she progressed in the field of medicine her genius became more and more apparent. In 1927, Professor Kleinschmidt, the Director of the Hamburg University Children's Clinic, in a testimonial letter necessary for admission to the specialty of Pediatrics wrote, "On account of her thorough preliminary knowledge of all branches of medicine and especially of internal medicine, it was possible to quickly grant her the necessary independence in the examination and treatment of sick children."

As time marched on and these shores were reached, some of the greatest doctors in New York saw in her a special luminary. In the words of Dr. Howard Schneider, an outstanding opthamologist: "Such a brain she had! She knew thousands of people, she remembered details of their lives, and she helped them through illness."

While Omi merited the accolades of her colleagues, it was her patients who benefited from her skill and saw her quality of modesty. Countless times after arriving at a difficult diagnosis she would say;

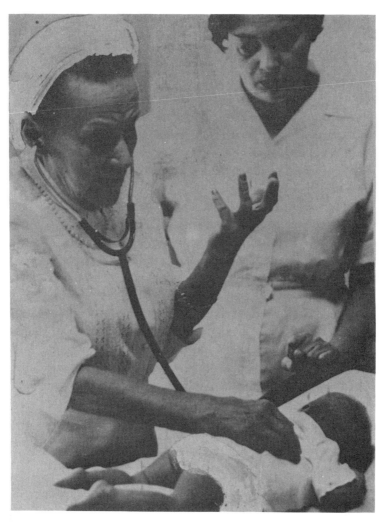

Dr. Wehl examining a baby

"Thank G-d, for diagnosis only comes from the Almighty." In truth she merited and did have *siyata d'Shmaya* (help from Above) in understanding what ailed her sick children. This Heavenly assistance enabled Omi to arrive at diagnoses that at times seemed far fetched and that were certainly not within the province of the average doctor.

As Rabbi Yaakov Fruchter eloquently said in his capacity as the chairman of the eulogy at the *sheloshim*, "When you came to Dr. Wehl with a child for an examination or for some piece of advice in time of distress, you knew that *siyata d'Shmaya* came along with whatever she had to say, not only because of her competence as a renowned pediatrician and diagnostician, but even more so because whatever she said came from a source of pure truth and integrity without any self-interest. Money meant nothing, it was not important; in fact the fees that she charged us recently were considered low even by the standards of twenty years ago. Her practice was conducted in a house steeped with *kedushah* (holiness) with large *mezuzos* guarding each door. Is there any wonder that she had *siyata d'Shmaya?*'

Once a patient brought a child, who was running a high fever, into the office for Omi to examine. After examining the child Omi found no visible symptoms to warrant such high fever. Omi had the feeling that this fever was an allergic reaction to an animal, and so she inquired if there were any pets in the house. The mother answered quite definitely in the negative: no animals, birds, or even fish. Diagnostic laboratory tests all resulted in negative findings. Yet Omi had a hunch and she insisted on pursuing it. A sample of the child's blood was sent to a special diagnostic laboratory in London, England. Sure enough the findings supported Omi's theory that this baby was allergic to some kind of animal or bird. Upon further investigation on the part of the child's parents, it was discovered that one of the neighbors in the next house had a bird. The child was ill continuously until the family found another apartment and moved away from the neighbor with the bird.

Omi's keen sense of perception is reflected in this story which occurred when a cranky baby running 102° temperature was brought into the office. After examining the baby and not being able to find anything specifically wrong with the child, Omi was baffled for a minute. Suddenly the baby let out a piercing cry. The minute Omi heard that cry, she said, "I don't like that cry. The last time I heard such a cry was thirty years ago." Immediately she picked up the phone and contacted Dr. Fish, the outstanding pediatric neurologist at New York University Hospital. They arranged to have the child admitted to the hospital. The admitting doctor felt that there was nothing wrong with the child, so Omi had to persuade him to do a spinal tap on the baby. The results were positive; the child was suffering from spinal meningitis. One might say that if one always listens to a child's cry, then the Almighty provides the understanding that is needed to interpret it.

Omi's character included two traits that tend to be contradictory in most people. Usually when a person is willing to defer his own opinion to that of others, he can develop the kind of humility that never allows him to take a firm position when necessary. On the other hand, a person whose firm conviction does not allow him to budge can become so obstinate that he will never accept a point of view different than his own. Omi was able to combine both of these seemingly contradictory aspects of personality. She never felt ashamed or humiliated when consulting with a colleague, and she even went to the extent of placing international telephone calls to discuss serious problems with those to whose expertise she wished to be privy. Yet at the same time when she was firmly convinced of the accuracy of her point of view, 'Mount Everest' couldn't budge her. She was not afraid to take a stand, even going so far as to oppose the medical staff of a hospital with which she was not affiliated.

Omi's perseverance in obtaining an accurate diagnosis was a legend. "When my now eight-year-old daughter was born, she was two months premature. Her lungs were very underdeveloped and the doctors did not give me much hope for her survival. The chief pediatrician at the hospital where I gave birth concluded that my little baby was suffering from cystic fibrosis. I called up my own pediatrician, Dr. Wehl, and cried to her on the phone. She was very skeptical about that diagnosis. She claimed that the diagnosis was highly unlikely, knowing my family history and all my other children. Dr. Wehl was not affiliated with the hospital in which I had given birth. She, however, immediately came to see me and convinced the doctors there to permit her to examine the baby. Dr. Wehl concluded that the baby was suffering from premature baby's pneumonia, and that unless the medicine was changed she would not survive. With the help of the Almighty, the doctors listened to Dr. Wehl. Today my little girl is a thriving eight-year-old who is a year ahead of herself in school."

A mother told us. "My newborn baby had a cold. I felt that the baby's illness was becoming progressively worse. Everybody on the staff of the hospital insisted that there was nothing wrong with the infant. The doctor in charge of the neonatal nursery refused to accept the child into that special nursery for sick newborn infants. Yet the baby was not nursing, and Dr. Wehl always insisted that a baby who could not nurse was in serious danger. After several days of observation with no improvement, Dr. Wehl, herself came down to the hospital at nine o'clock at night. She called up the chief pediatrician of that hospital, who was very annoyed at receiving such a late call at his home. He said to her, 'I am sorry, Dr. Wehl, you are calling me in the middle of my supper.' At that point, Dr. Wehl answered him, 'I am sorry, *Sir*, that I disturbed you in the middle of your supper. However, I came to the hospital directly from my office. I, too, have not eaten my supper yet. This baby needs antibiotics.' After some give-and-take, the baby was given the antibiotics and thank G-d improved within twenty-four hours. The baby was able to come home within the week. Yes, Rabbi Wehl, you said at the funeral that your mother stood up to the biggest doctors. I don't know if this one was one of the biggest, but I certainly saw her stand up to him."

In the words of another patient: "She did not care what specialists thought of her. She chevied them and chased them, she irritated them and annoyed them, she insisted that they examine her patients. She did not mind that they laughed at her. She did not care if they thought she was overly cautious. She only knew that there was only one thing that was important and that was the welfare of her children."

'The whole is greater than the sum of its parts' is a well-known expression. At times, an incident that occurred in Omi's practice reflected upon all of her superior characteristics. A sick child, under the care of another pediatrician, was referred to Omi for consultation. The child had been scheduled for surgery by a renowned pediatric surgeon. The referral to Omi was made at nine o'clock in the evening. Omi, who was seventy-nine years old at the time, said, "I had a very difficult day in the office and I am about to go to sleep; however, I have never refused to see a sick child." The child was brought into the office within fifteen minutes and was examined by Omi. She then asked the mother, who at the time was pregnant, to take a seat in the waiting room. She discussed the situation with the father of the child and said, "Your wife is pregnant and I do not want her to become overly concerned and worried. Most other doctors would insist on hospitalization. In view of your wife's present condition, I would like to avoid that. I am now going to call the surgeon and discuss the case with him." She proceeded to do so. Naturally, the surgeon was quite upset but knowing Dr. Wehl and having confidence in her evaluation, he agreed to see the child late that night. The surgeon, after examining the child, said, "He really requires surgery in the hospital but in deference to Dr. Wehl, I will try a minor procedure in my office. I must tell you, however, that the chance of its success is one percent." When the patient returned to the surgeon's office for a follow-up examination, the surgeon looked at the mother and said, "This is Dr. Wehl's miracle."

At times, Omi's instinctive sixth sense saved not only the life of a child but also that of a parent. This was beautifully described in a letter received after the *shivah*. "The first incident that really saved our family happened in 1945. My brother was born March 9, 1945. My mother came home from the hospital about ten days later. She was not feeling well, but she assumed that it was due to the recent birth. After my brother's *bris milah*, Dr. Wehl came to the house to check him. As she took one look at my mother, she told her not to get out of bed. She diagnosed a blood clot and prescribed complete bed rest. She then went down to the corner drugstore to call my mother's doctor (we couldn't afford a phone in our home) to inform him of the situation. He came and confirmed the diagnosis; in fact the clot had already reached her lung. If it were not for Dr. Wehl's diagnosis, done purely altruistically, we would not have my mother today. We are forever grateful to Hashem for His act of saving my mother and for the wonderful emissary that He sent."

Despite the fact that Omi did not treat adults, there were many families who consulted Omi and who benefited from her knowledge. At times Omi even closed her office to rush over to some adult who was suddenly taken ill to ascertain that the correct medical attention was administered. To many of them she was the messenger of the Almighty due to whose care and concern life was extended ten, fifteen and sometimes thirty years. Her greatness was evidenced by the fact that all this was done in such a unique and humble manner. Even the children of these people were often not aware of the lengths to which she went to preserve life. In fact, Omi treated four generations of some of the elite of American Jewry.

Some illustrations of her concern for the adults are mentioned below in quotations from letters we received after the *shivah* was completed.

"Dr. Wehl was not merely our pediatrician, but she was also our medical advisor. If we needed any help in choosing a specialist even for ourselves we never hesitated to ask her, and she was always most helpful. When my husband had a thyroid condition, Dr. Wehl was asked for her opinion and she steered my husband to the most renowned specialist in the city. He not only was a top man in his field but was also tops in character and modesty."

❊ ❊ ❊

"I had a procedure done in a hospital, and was told that radical surgery might be necessary. I was upset, as I felt that this might not really be so. Whom should I consult? Before even going home, or to my mother or sister, I went to Dr. Wehl. I knew she would listen and understand, and help me in any way she could. Dr. Wehl immediately contacted another doctor for a second opinion. She persuaded the hospital to release the slides for me, (which they usually don't do) so that I would't have to go through the tests again. It turned out that nothing further needed to be done. Dr. Wehl said to me, 'You are lucky you checked with someone else.' I replied, 'Thanks to you.' She said, 'It's not me, Hashem helped you.' "

❊ ❊ ❊

"One *Yom Tov*, early in the morning, an adult member of our family discovered an immobilizing growth. It was Dr. Wehl who rescued his *simchas Yom Tov* with a correct and brave diagnosis."

❊ ❊ ❊

Her dedication to her patients complemented her great memory and vice versa. Thus it was not unusual for Omi to recall the medical history of a child many years after the fact had long been forgotten. A former patient of Omi's once came over and introduced herself. Thereupon Omi asked her about the welfare of her son and recalled to her how as an infant he had a problem adjusting to dairy products. The mother smiled at Omi's ability to recall a condition that had already been corrected for more than twenty years.

❊ ❊ ❊

In casual conversation a famous educator recalled Omi's extraordinary powers of retention. When his daughter was ill with an ear infection Omi came to the house to examine the child. She assured his wife that there really was nothing to be concerned about because ear infections were common in the family. In fact, she recalled that the baby's uncle was brought into her office twenty-five years previously with just such an infection on the very same side. The father could not resist calling up his mother-in-law to verify this piece of information and to his utmost surprise it was exactly the way Omi had said.

❦ ❦ ❦

"As a child I was Dr. Wehl's patient. However, when I married and had my own children I used a different pediatrician. When one of my sons had pneumonia two-and-one-half years ago, my mother wanted Dr. Wehl, the expert, to examine him. My mother and I took him to her on a *motzaei Shabbos*. Dr. Wehl listened to his chest and heard a great deal of congestion. She looked up at my mother and said, 'Whose chest is this? Who had the same chest?' My brother, whose chest she hadn't listened to in twenty-five years! But years were of no meaning to Dr. Wehl. She remembered the sound of a chest which she hadn't heard in twenty-five years. Dr. Wehl was truly an unbelievable person and will be missed by all."

❦ ❦ ❦

A young bride-to-be came in for a last minute check-up before her marriage. Nothing unusual showed up in her examination. In the course of conversation Omi asked her if there were any specific problems that she had. The young lady told Omi that only one item caused her a slight degree of concern. This item was a recurring pain in a knee. This struck a bell with Omi. Thereupon she checked her records and sure enough her recollection was correct. She had treated the young lady nine years earlier for pain in a knee. Amazingly, both the girl and her mother could not remember seeing Omi for such a condition, yet Dr. Wehl did!

❦ ❦ ❦

Elsewhere we have referred to Omi's category of Shabbos and *Yom Tov* patients. There were among them some who took advantage of her willingness to help out in time of need. Yet her memory would not allow them to deceive her. Thus a number of years ago, a slightly humorous incident occurred on Pesach. A distraught father needing a doctor for his child on *Yom Tov*, and not being able to obtain the services of his own pediatrician, appeared at Omi's door. He said that he had just moved into the neighborhood and had, as yet, not chosen a pediatrician for his children. Thereupon Omi, recognizing the name and address of the gentleman, said to him, "You were in my office on this same *Yom Tov* five years ago. You live on the third floor, and if you want me to, I will even describe the furniture in your living room. The father, dumbstruck, apologized profusely for his forgetfulness and then thanked Omi for taking such excellent care of his child once again.

There were times when Omi had to remember weeks and months of diagnoses just to be able to recall to which patient she had given a particular medicine. Certainly if a child was allergic to some substance this was always uppermost in her mind. This ability not only aided the patient and the pharmacist but at times proved to be a life saver, particularly when a situation arose when a drugstore was unavailable. A patient came to Omi desperately on the night of Shemini Atzeres, during the last year of her life. It was late in the evening and the child required a certain medication. No pharmacy was open. Omi instantly went through her "computerized" patient list and tried to recall all those children who recently had used that specific medication. She then had to determine who might have some of the medicine left. After a moment or two she told the father of the child, "You are in luck and you only have to go right around the corner to the X-family. They should have enough of a supply left to last you through the two days of *Yom Tov*."

❧ ❧ ❧

When a boy puts on *tefillin* at the age of thirteen he stresses the fact that the *tefillin* on his head should enable him to understand "that the soul that is in my brain together with my other senses and potentials may all be subjugated to His service." Omi's phenomenal mind was indeed subjugated to His mission, the task of being a *Rofeh Choleh Amo Yisrael* (He Who heals the sick of His people, Israel).

CHAPTER 11

Twenty-Four Hours on Call

"The Aishes Chayil Award hanging over my desk will increase my feeling of responsibility to the welfare of my patients in the community."

his statement was written by Omi on April 28, 1977, the Monday after she was honored at the beautiful Sarah Schenirer High School and Teachers' Seminary Dinner. Omi rarely received the appropriate recognition that was due her, nor did she seek it. But at the strong suggestion of her dear friends and patients, Mr. and Mrs. Alfred Stern, who felt that the community owed it to her for her "responsibility for the lives of thousands of Jewish children — caring, loving, and rearing them only as a Jewish mother can ... and adhering to the principles of the Torah and character of our Matriarchs despite the formidable pressures and tribulations encountered throughout the years," Omi accepted the role of guest of honor.

This dinner gathered together hundreds of people who used the occasion to show their admiration for a true *Aishes Chayil* (woman of valor). One of the highlights of the evening was the presence of Rebbetzin Chanah Perel Kotler, the illustrious widow of the revered *rosh yeshivah* Rabbi Aharon Kotler. When she was asked by a close friend how it was possible for her to leave the Chinuch Atzmai Annual Dinner and attend this affair for Dr. Wehl, she replied, "Dr. Wehl left her home many a time to come to mine, whether it was day or night." In fact Mrs. Lezer, one of Omi's nurses, reminded us just recently of the fact that no matter how crowded the office was, and

Beth Jacob
Sara Schenirer
High School
Teachers Seminary
Proudly presents this
AISHIS CHAYIL AWARD
to
Dr. Selma Wehl, M.D.
*for her dedication and devotion to our institution and
to the Jewry of The Boro Park Community.
Dr. Wehl has given selflessly of her time and her energy for
these past thirty-eight years, and has thereupon won
the admiration and friendship of thousands.*

אשת חיל מי ימצא...

*Presented at the Tenth Anniversary Dinner - Brooklyn, New York,
April 24, 1977 -* ו' אייר תשל"ז

*Dr. Wehl speaking at the
Sara Schenirer H.S. dinner
in her honor*

despite Rebbetzin Kotler's protests, Omi would see her immediately whenever she brought her grandchildren to the office. Their relationship was remarkable. They represented two different worlds of Torah thinking; the Eastern European philosophy of *limud haTorah* (learning Torah) and the orthodox German philosophy of *Torah im derech eretz*. Yet they had the highest regard for each other. As a good friend of the family remarked, "No one who saw these two giants greeting each other will ever forget that moment."

It was not only the great giants who received Omi's undivided attention. In the most beautiful and eloquent eulogy at the *sheloshim* of Omi, Dr. Meir Schick movingly expressed what many people felt, by saying, "I believe it fair to say, however, that the *chesed* (loving-kindness) as a doctor, as a Jew, that she showed to Rabbi Aharon Kotler's grandchildren and great-grandchildren and other outstanding people was the same *chesed* she showed to anonymous people, people without the same credentials, but with sick children who had to be cared for."

A book on Omi illustrating her overriding quality of concern would read like an encyclopedia. We felt that it was important to mention some of the literally hundreds of stories that come to mind; not to do so would be unjust both to her and to the reader.

The average person attending a *bar mitzvah* or wedding usually plans to spend the evening in a relaxed and enjoyable fashion. Having had the privilege of driving Opi and Omi to many *simchos*, I always found it necessary to have change in my pocket. The minute Omi arrived at the hall, her first order of business was to check with her 'service.' This was invariably followed by return phone calls to patients, or on many occasions an immediate about-face and departure from the affair. Barely wishing a *mazel tov* to the parties involved, with no time for any socializing, Omi would be on her way back to see a sick child. This was the case even if it was a family gathering.

"My son was five years old in 1958 when he developed measles. He had high fever and Dr. Wehl had told me to keep her informed about his condition. It was *motzaei Shabbos,* about ten p.m. when my son complained that he could not move his head. I realized that this condition could be very serious, but I hesitated to call Dr. Wehl because of the lateness of the hour. The seriousness of the situation, however, prompted me to phone her office. I reached the answering service and was told that the doctor was out for the evening. I explained the situation to them; it wasn't more than ten minutes later that I received a return call from the doctor. Subsequently, I found out that Dr. Wehl had been in Riverdale, at a family *simchah.* That had not made a difference to her; in one hour she was at our house, examining my son. She wanted to see if he could walk, bend his head, etc. Thanks to the Almighty, it all turned out well. Her total dedication was unbelievable."

Day or night, Shabbos or Yom Tov, winter or summer, made no difference to Omi. She was so overworked that vacations were essential, not just a luxury for her. Yet even after Omi finally agreed to go away for several days of well-deserved rest, she still remained at the beck and call of her patients. Once when Omi already had her suitcases placed in the trunk of the car for a respite in the Catskill Mountains, she heard the phone ringing as she walked out the door. Despite the fact that her phone had been placed on service, she intercepted the call. A patient staying in Far Rockaway for the summer (one hour from Omi's home) called to obtain advice regarding a sick child. Omi gave her the necessary instructions and also gave her a telephone number where she could be reached, if necessary. Shortly, as the mother was tending to her sick child, there was a knock on the door. Who else but Dr. Wehl appeared to personally check the child! The patient felt terrible, knowing that Far Rockaway was in the opposite direction of the route to the mountains. The three-hour delay and the efforts involved, however, produced a lasting friendship between Joe and Lillian Wechsler and the Wehl family.

Rarely would Omi allow herself that luxury of going away for a Shabbos. On one such occasion she felt that she needed a break from her regular routine and agreed to spend a Shabbos in Long Beach. However, even this little change of routine did not come to fruition. Immediately upon her arrival in Long Beach, she received a phone call from one of her patients informing her that one of her children was running a very high fever. She assured the mother that the fever would go down and that the child would have a full recovery. Despite that, Omi felt that she could not enjoy Shabbos in Long Beach and returned home immediately, arriving right before the onset of Shabbos.

The elements of nature were no hindrance to Omi. Whether it was a downpour during a Shabbos walk or a snowstorm which made driving almost impossible, Omi managed to get there. One patient recalls, "It was a Friday. My youngest child was four weeks old and New York City was in the midst of a heavy snowstorm. My then five-year-old woke up with several small blisters. I suspected chicken pox and called Dr. Wehl to ask her advice. Dr. Wehl's diagnostic radar was instantly activated. Her concern was not primarily for the child with the chicken pox, but for my infant. She felt if the baby caught the chicken pox at her age, she might risk harmful side effects.

She asked that I bring both children to the office so she could make her diagnosis, and, if it was indeed chicken pox, she would give the baby a gamma globulin shot. We don't own a car and the snow was coming down heavily, so I was somewhat reluctant to venture out. Nevertheless, I said I'd try to get a car service and if I did, I would bring the children to the office. Before I could hang the phone up, Dr. Wehl told me to wait. She would get hold of a driver and would be over in a few minutes. Before I could protest, she hung up. Within fifteen minutes, she was at my house, had diagnosed chicken pox, and gave the baby a shot. When this took place, Dr. Wehl was almost eighty years old."

Omi would often say that being a pediatrician is not a nine-to-five job. One cannot program a child as to when he or she gets sick, nor can a tape-recording machine provide advice to a distraught mother. Indeed, she practiced what she preached. Thus it is no wonder that the following letters, which demonstrate an obvious consistent pattern of behavior, came to us after the *shivah* for Omi.

" ... At three weeks of age our daughter developed a severe stomach virus during the night. It seemed terrible to call a doctor in the middle of the night (this was our first child). However, having no choice, we did call Dr. Wehl. To our surprise, Dr. Wehl herself answered the telephone. She asked my husband to bring a soiled diaper to her house. She then told him to return with another soiled diaper, and then another, and to continue doing this until she was convinced what the problem was. This continued until four a.m. in the morning. She called a car service and sent my husband to an all-night pharmacy. She lent him the money for the car service and the medication. She then called me at home to tell me not to worry about my husband and told me his whereabouts. When we brought the baby in the next day to have her examined, we tried to pay Dr. Wehl for the previous night. She would take no more than the fee of that day's office visit."

" ... The story at hand took place when my son was approximately three months old. Unaware that my son could turn himself over, my wife, while grabbing for a diaper, left him on a dressing table for a split second. My son rolled off the table, which was approximately three-and-one-half feet high, and landed on the wooden floor. He had a tremendous bump on his head and did not appear to focus properly. My wife was crying hysterically, barely able to hold the baby. Having suffered greatly after giving birth, she had just built up enough strength to care for the baby and now this had happened. Dr. Wehl was immediately called. I had a speaker phone and remember hearing both ends of the conversation. With great skill, Dr. Wehl addressed all the necessary questions to diagnose the situation, while at the same time alleviating my wife's fears of any wrongdoing. She took great care to comfort the mother, while professionally providing all necessary instructions to monitor the status of the child. I am fortunate that I have a constant reminder of Dr. Wehl, for as I watch my son grow, I will always feel a debt of gratitude and appreciation for the care she provided for him and for the role model she provided for us."

" ... When our son was born, he came home from the hospital with a bad infection on his chin. Dr. Wehl said he would need frequent antibiotic injections so that the infection wouldn't spread through his system. She wouldn't trust anyone but herself to administer these injections. Dr. Wehl would drive to our home during the days, evenings, and even the middle of the night in order to treat him and check on his progress. She couldn't have cared more if our son had been her own child."

A father had been monitoring the progress of his sick child and decided to stay in the hospital through the night. At one a.m. he happened to be standing near the nurses' station when he heard the telephone ring. "Yes, Dr. Wehl, we are following your orders exactly," was the reply to the person on the phone. Finally at three-thirty a.m. the father went home to get an hour or two of sleep before the next day's work. On his way to *shul*, at six a.m. he stopped into the hospital to see how his child was progressing. As he was about to ask the nurse how things were, she said to him, "Don't worry, Mr. K., Dr. Wehl already called at five this morning to check everything out." The father added, "Your mother was in her eighties when this took place."

" ... My son Elchanon was hit on his head while playing baseball in the park. He was admitted to the hospital that evening. My husband was quite ill at the time. Dr. Wehl insisted that I go home to be with my husband and she would stay the night with my son."

" ... In my seventeen years of knowing Dr. Wehl, I only woke her up once in the middle of the night. My son seemed to be having breathing difficulties and I was distraught. Although it was one a.m., Dr. Wehl told me to come right over and was waiting for me at the door. She appeared more alert and awake than I was; she was seventy-nine years old at the time. She sent me to the hospital with my child and was in constant touch with me during the hours that I was there."

" ... Because out first child was born with a problem, Dr. Wehl made us promise to notify her as soon as my wife went into labor with our second child. The contractions began in the afternoon and Dr. Wehl arrived at the hospital even before we did. It turned out to be false labor, so we all went home. That night, around one or two a.m., the contractions began again and my wife was admitted to the hospital. I really didn't want to bother Dr. Wehl, but I knew she would be truly upset if I didn't call her. My phone call woke her up and she came to the hospital to stay with my wife until the baby was delivered and examined. Even though there had been no evidence of a problem in labor or delivery with our first child, Dr. Wehl wanted to do everything possible to assure us of a healthy baby this time. And she didn't even accept payment for being with my wife the whole night."

The idea of Omi's concept of 'daytime' was expressed most beautifully by Dr. Meir Schick. "In the modern period we have become subjugated to time, enslaved by it, and that enslavement progresses and it progresses most in the professions. We now have lawyers who no longer bill by the hour, nor the half of the hour, nor the quarter of the hour but rather by a tenth of an hour. Dr. Wehl went back to the heritage of being a doctor as described in the famous letter detailing the Rambam's weekly schedule. In it we find that day and night merged in the service of his patients. So too was our Dr. Wehl. She was a doctor one o'clock in the morning, five o'clock in the morning, and she could not sleep if she did not know what ailed the child. It was not three o'clock in the morning for her. She was lost in terms of time. She could not organize her duties as a Jewess or as a doctor in that fashion. As naturally as another doctor would have hours during the day for patients to call and to come in, Dr. Wehl would have hours anytime, day or night, to deal with the needs of her patients."

We make many requests to the Almighty in our prayers. In our fast day *Shemoneh Esrei* prayers we say טֶרֶם נִקְרָא אֵלֶיךָ עֲנֵנוּ (before we call to You, answer us). It is difficult for human beings to emulate their Creator, even though it is our obligation to do so. In a certain limited sense, Omi had this great virtue of not standing on ceremony to wait for the patient to call her. In fact her patients knew quite well that if they did not call at the appointed time, they could rest assured that their phone would be ringing with Dr. Wehl on the other end. A close friend of the family tells:

" . . . Our family was a croupy family. Dr. Wehl spent many nights in our house monitoring the welfare of our children. Not one of them surprised us by not getting croup. One morning I called her at six a.m. and apologized for waking the doctor. Boy, did I get it. 'What did you say! You were ready to risk the life of your child and not wake me. What do you think is more important, your child's life or my sleep? Never do that again; I'll be right over.' The next morning I really got it. I didn't report at seven a.m. as to how my son was feeling. I overslept since my alarm did not ring. Sure enough, at seven o'clock the phone rang. Dr. Wehl was on the job as usual. She told me that while I, the mother, might not be worried, she, the doctor, was."

A distinguished scholar was spending Shabbos in Boro Park, visiting his mother. His son had had a problem with his knee and it was impossible for the child to walk. Nothing and no one seemed to be able to help him. One of the father's relatives suggested that he call Dr. Wehl, who had been his own pediatrician. Omi suggested to him that he come visit her *motzaei Shabbos* with his son. After speaking to the child, Omi ascertained that the child had fallen from a bicycle. This, however, did not explain the child's inability to walk. She asked the father if the child had had a cold during the previous six weeks. The father replied in the affirmative. Omi then explained to him the medical ramifications of the combination of these symptoms. She prescribed a certain medication for the child and instructed him to stay in bed for twenty-four hours. She added that after twenty-four hours the child would be fully recovered. Omi asked the father to call her back at nine o'clock Sunday night. As he went to the phone to call Omi, his phone rang. It was nine o'clock, and the caller was none other than Omi. "Tell your son to get off the bed and let him walk around the room," directed Omi. It was exactly as she had predicted;

the child was fully recovered. The father then asked Omi how much he owed her for her services. She replied, "I told you to come visit me *motzaei Shabbos*. I do not charge for social calls."

Initiating a phone call was not only something that one might interpret as creating goodwill with a patient who was at present using Omi. Omi's determination to follow through no matter what, be it a patient or otherwise, was widely known.

" ... My first encounter with Dr. Wehl took place several years ago. It was a wintry *motzaei Shabbos* when my young baby woke up with a severe croup attack. Not being able to reach our own doctor, I was encouraged to telephone Dr. Wehl, who told me to come in immediately. This was a *motzaei Shabbos*, and I specify, I was not yet a patient of Dr. Wehl. The concern I was shown was phenomenal. I failed to report the child's condition the following morning and that warranted a telephone call from Dr. Wehl herself. Needless to say we had found a new family pediatrician."

" ... It was ten-and-a-half years ago when we first met Dr. Wehl. My oldest child had been running a fever for a couple of days and I was using a very prominent pediatrician. I had called him and he never returned my call. The baby was getting worse and my mother said to me, 'You have a doctor right next door. Please go and see her.' I was lucky; I did have Dr. Wehl right next door and I brought my baby to her to be examined. She examined the baby and told me she wanted to see her again. Of course, I was a new mother and I was going to stick with my own doctor. The next day, Friday morning, Dr. Wehl called me and asked me if I had spoken to my doctor. I tried to call and the answering service asked if it was an emergency. I said I didn't think so, and so the doctor never returned my call. Over the weekend the baby still had fever and was very weak and wasn't eating anything. Early Sunday morning, Dr. Wehl called me again, and mind you, I was not her patient. She asked me again if I had been in touch with my doctor. It was impossible to reach him; I tried again and again but to no avail. Dr. Wehl called me again and told me in a determined manner to bring the child to her office immediately. When I arrived at Dr. Wehl's office, there was nobody there at that time. The doctor examined the child and said to me, 'This child is very sick. I am calling a car service for you to take the child to the hospital, and I am calling the neurologist to meet you at the hospital to administer a spinal tap.' I was reluctant to go. I said, 'My husband is not here.' She pointed to the telephone and said, 'Call him, tell him to come right over.' My husband came and before I knew it, there was a car waiting for us. We arrived at the hospital and the neurologist was waiting for us because Dr. Wehl had called him and told him to meet us. The baby was examined and the spinal tap was done. The doctor came out to tell us that the baby had meningitis and was very sick. We thank Hashem for directing us to the right emissary and we are indebted to Dr. Wehl. Without her determination, who knows what the end result would have been."

Her deep concern supplemented by her *siyata d'Shmaya* at times produced what chassidic rabbis might call a miraculous event. In the later years it was customary for the mother of a newborn infant, who was born in an out-of-Boro Park hospital, to immediately bring the infant to the office for a thorough examination. One patient of Omi's gave birth in a very prestigious hospital immediately preceding the summer vacation. She did not bring in her baby to the office. Omi personally called her and reminded her of this practice. As a matter of courtesy, the patient acceded to Omi's demand and brought the ten-day-old child to the office on Thursday. After the completion of the examination, Omi said, "I want to tell you two things. First of all, I now know your baby. Secondly, if a problem should arise, Dr. X in Monticello is a very capable doctor." After wishing each other a *guten Shabbos* the patient was on her way to the country. The following Shabbos the baby did not seem to be acting the way that a healthy twelve-day-old baby should. The parents contacted both Omi and the local doctor. The baby was hospitalized. The child had spinal meningitis, a very serious disease for such a young child. Omi conducted the medical care of the child via the telephone and was in contact with the local doctor and hospital the whole Shabbos. The baby recovered. The father, a prominent Torah scholar, is to this day astounded by the *siyata d'Shmaya* involved.

Not only was Omi available to patients and non-patients during her 'free time,' but at times Omi would stop everything to go and see a sick child. There were numerous occasions when a full waiting room of patients was called upon to join in Omi's sacred mission. When an emergency situation arose, Omi would leave the office on a moment's notice. The nurse would inform the patients that an emergency had arisen and that the the doctor would be back as soon as possible. She moved with such haste that it was hard for all to realize what was happening.

"... My son suddenly became very ill. It seemed to us that he had trouble moving. He was lying in bed in a situation that was certainly most frightening for us as young parents. I called Dr. Wehl. She had a full office. She said to me, 'Mrs. X, I am closing the office. I'll be there in ten minutes.' Personal friends of ours who sat in the office at the time attested to her flying out of her consultation room saying, 'I have an extremely ill patient. I am sorry I must close my office.' She raced out the door. Thanks to the Almighty, the situation resolved itself within an hour or two. The child was suffering from a case of pneumonia. During the period of time that Dr. Wehl did not know what was wrong with this child, he was the only thing that mattered. Until she could set her mind at ease and know that he was not in any danger, everything else was put on a back burner."

Omi's total *hisbatlus* (total lack of self-consideration) was discussed by Rabbi Yaakov Fruchter. "Dr. Wehl displayed total *hisbatlus* when being involved with her patients. She knew that she was G-d's messenger to help others. She lived up to that Talmudic principle of a messenger carrying out his mission in its fullest sense of the word. When involved with a patient, her personal comforts meant nothing. She did not count. It was the patient's well-being that counted, nothing else — total *hisbatlus*. When one called upon her in the middle of the night with trepidation no recording was heard to tell one to call back in the morning, but rather an alert voice gave one instructions about what to do. Instead of anger, she calmed us by saying that she was not sleeping anyway, and that we had done the correct thing by calling. Yes, פִּיהָ פָּתְחָה בְחָכְמָה (*she opens her mouth with wisdom*), but at the same time תּוֹרַת חֶסֶד עַל לְשׁוֹנָהּ (*a lesson of kindness was on her tongue — Mishlei 31:26*). These two, *chachmah* and *chesed*, went hand in hand with Dr. Wehl. When she felt a patient needed hospitalization at any hour, she alerted the hospital staff and a team was waiting when one arrived. This situation could have repeated itself a number of times each week, even when she was in her late eighties. It was not a rarity that Dr. Wehl herself appeared at the hospital soon after, or that she was on the telephone the rest of that night finding out what the condition of the child was. Total *hisbatlus.''*

At the time that Omi herself was hospitalized, we came to visit her late one night, at which time an administrator in charge of admissions called us aside. He asked us if we were aware of Omi's distinct and unique character as a doctor. He continued by saying, "Your mother is different: when she sends a baby into the hospital at three o'clock in the morning, she is usually here by three-thirty."

This total involvement with the welfare of a patient brings to mind an incident that occurred about twenty years ago, in which we were personally involved. It was our habit to visit Opi and Omi every single Shabbos. On one such occasion, when we arrived, Opi seemed quite worried. Omi had left for a house call three hours earlier. Opi, neither using nor answering the telephone, had no way of knowing what was transpiring. He asked us if we would kindly walk over to the patient's house to ascertain if anything unusual had occurred. Upon arriving at the patient's home, we explained the purpose of our visit. The mother of the child apologetically remarked, "I am sorry that we disturbed your father's Shabbos, but I must tell you that while your mother was here, there was nothing on her mind but the health of my little baby. It was only after caring for the child that she became aware of the time element involved."

We have heard many stories, tales, and anecdotes during these last few months. Countless times Omi's devotion prevented a critical situation from developing. Many people expressed this in many ways. In 1975 Omi received the following letter.

> Dear Dr. Wehl:
>
> Last weekend, November 1st, I celebrated my thirty-first birthday. Many thoughts went through my mind at the time. I thought about my first birthday, thirty years ago. I thought about the fact that, if not for you, I don't think I would have lived through my first birthday, much less any of those that followed.
>
> My first birthday, as I'm sure you recall, took place in the hospital. It was only through your sense of dedication and professional expertise, and with the help of the Almighty, that I was able to survive a most serious threat to my life. I have never forgotten you for this. I often times forget the faces of people I met last week, but although I haven't seen

you in many years, I have never forgotten your face. I now am the rabbi of a wonderful *shul*, the husband of a lovely wife and the father of two wonderful boys. You, in large part, made it all possible.

Our Sages tell us, "He who saves a soul is as though he saved a universe." Well, you saved my life and the lives of many others. For this, I am eternally grateful.

I hope and pray that the Almighty will grant you and your family good health and *nachas* so that you may continue to serve the Almighty and mankind "with all your heart, and with all your soul and with all your might."

CHAPTER 12

Integrity at Its Utmost

"One thing I can tell you, you will never see a patient of mine."

he above statement was delivered under conditions which required great *mesiras nefesh* (self-sacrifice). Only Omi who had such a high degree of integrity and courage would have responded so quickly and so much to the point. In 1943, when Omi opened her office in Boro Park, an ear, nose, and throat specialist called and asked her to recommend him to her patients. In the process of his conversation he suggested that Omi could expect remuneration for every patient she would send to him. This procedure was called fee splitting and the suggestion by the specialist elicited the above response.

This incident was repeated frequently in one form or another. Omi saw two evils in fee splitting. Her feelings regarding this topic were best described here: "Once Dr. Wehl sent me to a skin specialist, who charged me a lower fee than usual. The nurse, wondering at the lower fee, was told by the doctor that since Dr. Wehl did not take money for recommending a patient, there was no need to charge the full rate. When I asked Dr. Wehl about it she said, 'I want to be honest and to do what is in the best interest of the patient. If I would take money, my judgment might be biased, and I might send the patient to the doctor who splits his fee, rather than to the one who is most competent. For the same reason,' Dr. Wehl continued, 'I give the money from Shabbos visits to charity because then I know that I will only go on a house call on Shabbos if it is really an emergency'.

Honesty and integrity of character were foremost on the list of Dr. Wehl's superior traits".

Mrs. Devorah Schechter, a dear friend of the Wehl family, in a most beautiful tape that was prepared with all the eloquence of a eulogy, said, "Dr. Wehl set rules. She had her ideas of what was right. She set unwavering standards for herself, and she could not understand how the rest of the world could not appreciate the pure simplicity of the uncomplicated system of ethics that was her credo. She had great difficulty accepting the grey areas of compromise. She could not come to terms with that which many of us have routinely come to expect as the price of modern living. Her uncompromising honesty and her unflinching determination to be a woman of integrity in a world clearly seduced by materialism and the easy dollar compelled her to speak out firmly for the old-fashioned values of sincerity and honesty."

Omi had a hatred for deceit. Her word, whether to members of the family or to a patient, was tantamount to a pledge. If she told a patient that she would remain in the city until her baby was born, nothing could alter that commitment. Thus, a patient who attended the *sheloshim* contributed the following remarks: "I am not a writer but I must mention two things that were not said at the eulogy. 'I could not go away during the month of August,' said Dr. Wehl. 'A few of my patients are giving birth and I must be there for them.' When I told her that I was expecting my baby at the end of the summer, she said she would certainly be back before then. Sure enough, I gave birth two weeks early. Dr. Wehl then commented, 'Wasn't it a good thing that I came back earlier?' "

Maimonides' prayer for the doctor permeated her actions. The Rambam (Maimonides) asks of Hashem, "that You give me the courage and impetus to do my work honestly and diligently, and that the desire to accumulate wealth or fame should not blind my path." She strove to live up to these ideals. Consequently, it is no wonder that Omi's concept of charging fees was a distinctly unique one. Literally thousands of incidents can testify to this.

One of Mrs. Rose Wasser's children had fallen in the house and was screaming and writhing in pain. She called Omi, who immediately came to the house. Upon examination, Omi determined that the arm was broken. Mr. Wasser was not available at that time so

Omi took mother and child to the office of a leading orthopedist and remained with her for the duration of the afternoon until her husband was able to get there. After returning home, Mrs. Wasser called Omi, to ask her the fee for her services. Omi's reply was, "Just the amount I take for an ordinary house call."

Another patient, whose baby's condition and treatment demanded that Omi be up most of the night, attempted to pay her for her all-night vigil. Omi responded by saying, "What can I charge you for half a night's sleep?" She then proceeded to take her regular office fee, not a cent more.

If a patient visited Omi a number of times in one week, she avoided charging for the subsequent visits. Sometimes she would even justify her not charging by putting the blame on herself. One incident made such an indelible impression on the ten-year-old daughter of Mrs. Fay Steinberg that she felt it necessary to write: "I had a rash and my father took me to Dr. Wehl on *motzaei Shabbos*. Dr. Wehl refused payment from my father. She said, 'The rash could have been there on Thursday, when you were last here, and maybe I did not recognize it.' " After Opi's passing away, there was not a Shabbos that Mrs. Steinberg did not visit Omi. If she could not come, for whatever the reason, she would call on *erev Shabbos* to wish Omi a *gut Shabbos*. This included a telephone call from London to Omi on the *erev Shabbos* that Mrs. Steinberg was visiting there.

Sometimes the difference between the fees charged by various doctors was literally astounding. A prominent *talmid chacham* personally told us the following incident. During a time when he was not using Omi as a doctor, his child was sick and had to be hospitalized for four days. The doctor charged him three hundred and fifteen dollars. Two years later when the cost of living had risen even higher he came to Omi's office. At that time, unfortunately, his child had a recurrence of the previous ailment. She was again hospitalized for four days. The father of the child told me, "Your mother made at least forty-five phone calls, and visited the hospital every day. What I want to tell you is that with difficulty we were able to persuade her to accept fifty dollars in payment for her services."

This was not unusual. *Bnei Torah* or others who could not afford the regular fee were charged a reduced fee or no fee at all. A young wife whose husband is still a Talmud student said, "I had the honor of having Dr. Wehl care for my first child while the baby was in the hospital. I could not afford to continue using her, so I took my baby to a Medicaid doctor. When my second child was born Dr. Wehl convinced me that I should use her. She explicitly requested that I come to her without payment. Doctor Wehl took care of six of my children with utmost care and motherly love, never requesting a fee. Once on a Tishah B'Av, while fasting, although advanced in years, Dr. Wehl came to the hospital to examine one of my children." People who knew Omi well were aware of the fact that fasting on Yom Kippur and Tishah B'Av was so difficult for her that she remained in bed all day. Yet when a patient needed her attention, an inner strength suddenly took over.

"And how about all the times when she knew how hard it was to eke out a living and so she would only take money from whatever my insurance paid? When I had no insurance she would take nothing. I have reason to believe that the most honest tax returns were those of Dr. Wehl's."

A patient of Omi was an eyewitness to an interesting episode. While sitting in the waiting room waiting for her turn, she noticed a very poorly dressed man bringing his four children in for an examination. As he left the consultation room, she heard him ask Omi about the fee. Omi answered, *"Gayt gezunterheit"* (go in good health). When the patient who had observed this incident mentioned something about it to Omi, her response was, "Sometimes, I too like to do a *mitzvah.*"

Not charging the patient the regular fee did not diminish Omi's concern and quality of medical attention. At times it was just the opposite. Once, on an *erev Shabbos*, Omi asked me for the telephone number of a particular patient. Since it was only ten minutes before the time of candle lighting, my immediate response was, "Omi, can't this phone call wait till after Shabbos?" Thereupon she replied, "This patient is not in the financial position to pay for my services. She was in the office yesterday. I asked her to keep me up-to-date about the child, but she has not called yet. Maybe, she does not want to bother me since I do not charge her. Therefore I must call her. She is no different than a paying patient. I cannot enter Shabbos in a peaceful state of mind unless I know how this child is doing."

Omi not only gave of herself, but because of both her own honesty and integrity and her concern for her patients, she was able to convince other doctors and specialists to charge her patients a reduced fee when needed. A famous educator in the Yeshivah Day School movement submitted the following to us. "When my daughter needed the service of an orthopedist, Dr. Wehl, knowing that our financial situation did not allow us the privilege of a specialist, personally called the specialist and requested special consideration for us."

A tape to us relates a mother's concern and the doctor's empathy. "As I dressed my second child, I noticed a lump on the right side of her neck. I was frantic, so I rushed the two-week-old baby to the doctor's office. Dr. Wehl immediately arranged for someone to drive us posthaste to the hospital to consult a distinguished specialist. She stayed with me until the specialist made the diagnosis that the child had a short muscle in her neck which needed certain remedial exercises. At a follow-up appointment at the specialist's office, his nurse greeted me by saying, 'You should know that Dr. Wehl just called us and as a result, we are extending a courtesy to you and charging you a reduced fee for both the hospital conference and this office visit.' Dr. Wehl did not take any money for either the visit to her office or for the transportation to the hospital, despite the fact that she hired the driver. She was so considerate, and she never thought about herself."

A number of years ago, I entered a noted local pharmacy to pick up a prescription for Omi and the pharmacist at the desk asked me, "Are you related to Dr. Wehl?" I replied in the affirmative. He said, "Let me tell you something about her. Six years ago she taught me a lesson that I will never forget. At that time I was employed by a different drugstore. I received a prescription for one of Dr. Wehl's patients. Since the store did not have the prescribed drug in stock, we substituted a similar one. Within fifteen minutes of the patient's departure from the store, Dr. Wehl was on the phone reprimanding me as follows, 'What right do you have to assume responsibility for the life of this child?' This particular type of 'substitution' had been done hundreds of times. Your mother was the first and only one who called to protest. I have never done that again." It is no wonder that on different occasions many patients presented Omi with Maimonides' Prayer on a plaque, for she incorporated so much of it into her own being.

Her honest way of life was most appropriately described by Rabbi Gershon Weiss at the eulogy at the *sheloshim:* "She was a real *mentsch*. A *mentsch* as Hashem wants one to be. She was careful about the *kashrus* of the medicine, and was careful about the *kashrus* of money. She wanted to make sure that her money was all *kosher*."

CHAPTER 13

The Total Picture

"My orders remain unchanged. No one is to touch the child until I know who the surgeon will be."

mi was not only a genius in the field of medicine, she had a heart of gold as far as her patients were concerned and was sensitive to many little things that one might normally overlook. She saw the whole child, both in his present situation and in terms of the future. The above quotation highlights the following incident.

A patient was taken to the emergency room and according to hospital policy, Omi, the patient's pediatrician, was notified. Realizing that the child might need a stitch or two, Omi asked the nurse in the emergency room which doctor was on duty. Omi did not know the doctor who was mentioned and so she told the nurse that no one should undertake any procedure on the child. The nurse became quite upset and said, "Dr. Wehl, what are you making such a big deal about? The child does not require twenty-five stitches; at the most one or two stitches is all that is needed." Omi then reiterated her point. In addition Omi requested that the father of the child be allowed to speak to her on the telephone. She told the father, "The nurse does not understand. Right now your daughter is three years old, but in time she will be eighteen. I want to make sure that the doctor who sutures her should not only be knowledgeable but also should be someone who can do it without leaving a scar on her face." Thinking about fifteen years in the future, when the girl's appearance would become an important factor in her life, was on

Omi's mind and of prime consideration at the time when the patient was yet a baby.

This tenderheartedness reflected itself in many other incidents. Many years ago a patient who had just given birth received a vase of flowers from Omi. The patient was surprised and when Omi came to examine her baby she expressed her astonishment. Omi responded, "I know your uncle passed away yesterday. I was sure that the family was busy with the funeral, and I did not want your happy event to go unnoticed. I wanted you to have these flowers to brighten the day that you would be spending alone in the hospital."

Much has already been written about Omi's visitations to the hospital and the devotion that they required. It was not only the medical aspects of a case that brought Omi to the hospital. At times it was the human element that forced her to be there, and to remain there for a considerable amount of time, as this letter clearly expresses. "When my son was operated on for an infected appendix, Dr. Wehl came to the hospital during the night in order to be present during the operation. I said, 'Dr. Wehl, you did not have to come at night.' She replied, 'I know it makes you feel better if I am around. You know me, but the surgeon is a stranger to you.' How right she was! What a comfort it was to me that Dr. Wehl was there. She came out to me every couple of minutes to reassure me that everything was going well. At the end of the operation she said, 'If you wait a while the surgeon will talk to you.' I waited and talked to him. As I was preparing to leave the hospital I saw Dr. Wehl standing outside and waiting for me. I asked her why she was still there at three o'clock at night. She answered, 'I am going to drive you home. How else can you get home at night?' (This was before the days of car services)."

"When I was fourteen years old I required emergency surgery late in the evening. As I was being wheeled on the stretcher towards the operating room, Dr. Wehl suddenly appeared at my side. As a response to my expression of surprise she said, 'I knew that I could not take the place of your parents but I felt that you would be happy to see a familiar face here. I will remain with you throughout the whole operation.' Needless to say, she did".

At times this sensitivity involved third parties becoming accomplices to her concern for her patients' welfare. Mrs. S. recounted: "It was ten-thirty at night. I had had a rough day and was happy to be able to get to sleep early. The phone rang and I hoped I wouldn't get tied up on the telephone. I was shocked when I heard Dr. Wehl's voice at the other end. Why would Dr. Wehl be calling me? I hadn't recently had a baby; none of the children was ill. I knew Dr. Wehl always called after I had a baby to see how we were managing. This, of course, was usually after she had sent flowers in honor of the occasion. But why was she calling me now? I soon was enlightened. We lived in a large apartment house. Dr. Wehl called to tell me that there was a young mother in the building who was alone with her sick baby at that hour of the night. The baby was running a very high fever and Dr. Wehl had instructed the mother to sponge the child. The doctor called me to ask me to go up to this young mother's apartment to help her with her sick child and keep her company. Where could one find a pediatrician, or any doctor for that matter, who cared so much for her patients?"

One of the most crucial moments in a young woman's life is the time of the delivery of a newborn baby. Omi was not an obstetrician, so theoretically she had nothing to do with the delivery. Her role began after the baby was born. Yet countless patients recall how she was always there for them in times of need. Omi's 'antennae' always alerted her to know just where she should be and when she should be there. Sometimes the natural 'beeper' would sound months before birth, and at other times not until the night of delivery. Her strong empathy for an expectant mother was invaluable.

"Dr. Wehl's greatness was not only in her medicine, but it also lay in the fact that she was an unbelievable *mentsch.* I recall that when I was expecting my third child I had to remain in bed for the last few months of my pregnancy and I was very depressed. My sister had an appointment in Dr. Wehl's office, and during the course of conversation told the doctor about my plight. The following Shabbos there was a knock on my door. Lo and behold, there was Dr. Wehl, already in her eighties. She came in, sat down and talked to me. I told her how very hard and difficult this ordeal was for me. She looked at me, smiled, and said, 'Don't ever say that. Nothing is hard. We can do everything if we want to.' I am sure that this was her philosophy in her own life."

There were times when not even the patient was aware of her concern. Rather Omi would bear the brunt of the worry herself. Only after the problem was fully solved might the patient know of its gravity. A patient writes that in 1978, while she was expecting her third child, she had to undergo surgery. Omi never uttered a word about her concern for the unborn baby. On the contrary she gave the young mother all the encouragement she needed to overcome her worries. Omi was in the delivery room immediately after the birth of the baby. She told the mother that the baby was perfectly fine. The mother wondered why Omi had appeared there so soon after delivery. Upon investigation she discovered that Omi was so deeply concerned that she had left word in the hospital that she should be notified as soon as labor began. She was there to reassure the patient that all was well. The patient ends her letter, 'I'll never forget her words.'

Anyone who was privileged to have been Omi's patient knows how cautious she was. She certainly was very stringent in areas dealing with the saving of the life of a child. She would not hesitate to send one of her babies to another doctor for consultation. Nor would she desist from ordering both blood and other laboratory tests to 'play it safe.' She would say, "Nine hundred and ninety-nine times everything will be all right, but I am worried about the one case out of a thousand that doesn't go correctly." Despite that, there were times that her sensitivity to, and evaluation of, a particular case caused her to assume the major burden of responsibility herself. This was particularly true when the issue of hospitalization of a child had to be considered. Omi was hesitant to order quick hospitalization. She tried to keep the child at home as long as possible. These interesting situations reflect both on Omi's superior medical attention as well as on her humanitarian feelings.

"On another occasion Dr. Wehl's understanding and capacity to care for the whole family carried us through a difficult period. My one-year-old child had some sort of virus infection and was becoming dehydrated. She wasn't drinking, she was vomiting and she appeared listless. Dr. Wehl warned me that if she didn't start retaining any liquids soon she would have to be hospitalized to be fed intravenously. At the same time my father-in-law had fallen and had broken his hip. He was in the hospital, so my mother-in-law was staying with us. She was very worried and disturbed about my father-in-law and consequently we were trying to hide the fact that the baby was so sick. I was determined to keep the baby home if at all possible because I knew that my mother-in-law would be terribly upset if the baby was hospitalized as well. Shabbos was coming and Dr. Wehl suggested that I feed the baby with a medicine dropper, hoping that she would be able to retain minute amounts of liquid. Just before Shabbos I spoke to Dr. Wehl to give her the latest report on the baby. I was told to come over every two hours on Shabbos, to report on the situation. She would thus be able to determine when hospitalization might become absolutely necessary without endangering the child's life. It was wintertime and Shabbos started early in the evening. At eight p.m. my husband was knocking at Dr. Wehl's door. At ten p.m. he was back there again and she gave him a final deadline of one a.m. If the baby had not retained any liquid by then, she would have to be admitted to the hospital. At midnight the baby began moving around and drinking her bottle. The crisis passed and my mother-in-law never even knew what had taken place. All this was due only to the accurate and loving care of Dr. Wehl. She really cared. We always were aware of her devotion and we were very grateful to her."

"Dr. Wehl never chose the easy route for herself. When our six-week-old infant ran a high fever of 106° without symptoms of any infections we rushed over to her office. She immediately told us that we had to take the baby to the diagnostic laboratory for tests. She called the cab for me and then she called the laboratory demanding immediate attention for my baby. By the time I arrived back home from the laboratory, Dr. Wehl had already called me with the results of the tests. Although she was worried, to say the least, she had the courage and confidence not to rush the child to the hospital. She did not want to weaken the child with indiscriminate testing or disrupt a family. She felt that perhaps a symptom would show up the following morning, but she still stayed up the whole night worrying about our child, calling me every half hour until late into the night, and then again at six a.m. the next morning. When I returned to her office early in the day, to her relief and to ours, she discovered swollen glands."

Every Purim, among the many *shalach manos* on Omi's table, one could find a vase of beautiful flowers sent by Rabbi and Mrs. Yoel Kramer. This relationship of the Kramers to Omi started when Rabbi

Kramer was a youngster living in a small town which had no *yeshivah*. His parents sent him to live with his uncle and aunt, Rabbi and Mrs. Anshel Fink, in Boro Park, where he was able to attend *yeshivah*. He told us the following incident that occurred when he was a young teenager. "I fell ill with pneumonia at one a.m. on a *motzaei Shabbos*. Dr. Wehl came to see me immediately. She diagnosed my illness and remained at my bedside the entire night until the crisis had passed. When she was asked why she hadn't hospitalized me, despite the seriousness of my illness, she answered, 'Since the Finks were not the patient's natural parents, such a crisis and a move as traumatic as hospitalization would have been an undue strain on them.' She rationalized that if she stayed with me, she could monitor me medically, hospitalizing me only when no choice existed, thus protecting the Finks emotionally."

Rabbi Kramer described another episode that moved them intensely. "Dr. Wehl not only demonstrated her sensitivity during my illness, but many years later when my wife gave birth during the *Yom Tov* of Pesach, we had another experience which, although totally different in nature, reflected that same feeling of care for the total person. I woke the doctor at six-thirty that morning to share our good news with her. Within two hours, she was in the hospital, bringing with her a knife, an apple and a bar of chocolate. She felt that since it was Yom Tov, I might not be able to get to the hospital early and she was concerned that Judy should not remain hungry until I could bring her some food."

There really are limitless numbers of stories that can be told. Everything written here is just a drop in the ocean. It is difficult to really describe the intangibles. In *Shemoneh Esrei* we describe the Almighty as a faithful and a compassionate Healer. It seems that feelings of sympathy, empathy, and sensitivity to a patient's needs are an integral part of a true doctor. In the words put on a tape by the Kiwak-Halpern-Laufer sisters, "Dr. Wehl didn't only feel with her hands, she felt with her heart. She was a doctor with a world of feeling."

The eye chart Dr. Wehl used for yeshivah students

CHAPTER 14

One of a Kind

*"Don't take my word for it, set up an appointment in
Manhattan with one of the biggest specialists in that field."*

t takes one to know one" is a famous colloquialism.
Throughout Omi's lifetime she endeavored to keep up
with the latest medical information. She also made it her
business to associate with the most renowned and qualified doctors.
Even in her later years Omi did not feel it beneath her dignity to
attend lectures at the hospital. The lecturer may have been half her
age, and nowhere near as experienced as she, yet she always felt that
there was something to learn. She fulfilled the famous saying אֵיזֶהוּ
חָכָם? הַלּוֹמֵד מִכָּל אָדָם, *Who is wise? He who learns from every person*
(*Pirkei Avos 4:1*).

Sometimes Omi's attendance at a lecture gave her a keener insight
which ultimately served her patients' needs. The following was
related by a patient: "My child developed a swollen arm. It was *erev
Shabbos* and we wanted to take all the necessary precautions before
Shabbos began. We called Dr. Wehl, who, after examining our child,
told us that it was most probably an allergic reaction to a medication.
She pointed out that interestingly enough, she had been at a lecture in
the hospital the day before where they were reviewing such cases."

In all her years of practicing medicine, Omi never felt humiliated if
she consulted with another doctor. However, the one thing that she
did insist upon was that this doctor should be a leader in his specialty.
Thus it is no surprise that Omi developed contacts with leading
specialists in various fields. They, in turn, saw in Omi everything that

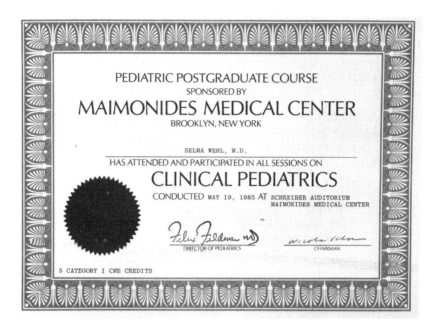

PEDIATRIC POSTGRADUATE COURSE
SPONSORED BY

MAIMONIDES MEDICAL CENTER
BROOKLYN, NEW YORK

SELMA WEHL, M.D.

HAS ATTENDED AND PARTICIPATED IN ALL SESSIONS ON

CLINICAL PEDIATRICS

CONDUCTED MAY 19, 1985 AT SCHREIBER AUDITORIUM
MAIMONIDES MEDICAL CENTER

DIRECTOR OF PEDIATRICS   CHAIRMAN

5 CATEGORY I CME CREDITS

a pediatrician should be. Dr. Doyle, a leading pediatric cardiologist at New York University Hospital, was overheard telling a group of interns and residents, in the presence of the mother of a child whom Dr. Wehl had sent to her for consultation, "This woman (pointing to the mother of the child) has a doctor who possesses every single characteristic that a doctor should have."

It should have been no surprise to us that one of America's leading neurologists, Dr. Irving Fish of New York University Hospital, closed his office and appeared anonymously at Omi's funeral. He was so awed by Omi's diagnostic skills and by her sincere devotion to her patients that on a number of occasions he had called Omi and arranged to come to her home to meet this 'amazing lady.' This meeting never took place however, because every time it was scheduled, Omi was too busy in her practice. On the morning when she passed away, a patient of Omi's was then in Dr. Fish's office, and she mentioned the dreadful loss that had occurred in our community. Instantly he called in his nurse, canceled his appointments and told the patient that he was taking her back to Boro Park, because he too wanted to attend the funeral and pay his respects to the doctor. In his humility, Dr. Fish did not introduce himself to us at the funeral. We only found out about his attendance there during *shivah*, when the patient made us aware of it.

Whether it was Dr. Joseph Pincus, the former Chief of Pediatrics at the Brooklyn Jewish Hospital, who would join Omi at consultations which usually began after twelve midnight and lasted into the early morning hours; or whether it was Dr. Umansky, the Chief of Orthopedics at the Joint Disease Hospital, who once held up an entire operating room for that 'little lady'; or whether it was Dr. Golinko, former Chief of Pediatrics at Brookdale Hospital, who came out late at night to see one of Omi's patients, and said, "The only one I would do this for is Dr. Wehl," or Dr. Murray Bess, a chief at Mount Sinai who admonished a patient for coming to see him after seeing Omi — all were in awe of that 'little lady.'

Indeed the words of our Sages אֵיזֶהוּ מְכֻבָּד? הַמְכַבֵּד אֶת הַבְּרִיּוֹת, *Who is honored? He who honors others (Pirkei Avos 4:1)* applied to Omi. As one of Omi's patients wrote, "Dr. Wehl, of blessed memory, was a woman who actually hated honor but she was very careful of the honor of everyone she knew, rabbis, noted physicians, parents and yes, even little children. It made no difference."

A mother complained to Omi that her nine-year-old son was a hypochondriac. Every week this child had something else to complain about, the back, the knee, the arm, the chest, etc. The mother made nothing of it. But as Dr. Howard Schneider said at the *sheloshim* for Omi, "She taught doctors the importance of *listening* to the patient." She always listened to the patient, so she listened to this little nine-year-old boy. She listened to all his complaints and followed through by taking all the steps and precautions medically necessary to find the answer to his aches. She finally recommended that this child be examined by an outstanding specialist. At first the specialist saw nothing wrong with the child. At Omi's insistence, however, the specialist agreed to conduct further tests. Due to the help of the Almighty and the determination on Omi's part, rheumatic fever was caught in its earliest stages, and today the child is perfectly healthy. Needless to say, this specialist's name joined the roster of Omi's admirers.

❧ ❧ ❧

What was it that all these doctors saw in Omi? Let their words speak for themselves.

As a young pediatrician Omi's talents were already noticed. When Omi was thirty-five years old, Prof. Dr. H. Kleinschmidt, Director of the Hamburg University Children's Clinic, wrote the following testimonial:

> Dr. Selma Lewin has received her training as a specialist for children's diseases at the University Children's Clinic in Hamburg, of which I was in charge at that time. After she had established herself I was frequently called in consultation to visit sick children together with her. On these occasions I very often had the opportunity to convince myself not only of her thorough medical knowledge, but also of the great attention and conscientiousness with which she took care of her patients. Miss Lewin never minded any time or trouble. In short, she devoted herself completely to her medical profession.

Dr. Howard Schneider, one of the leading eye specialists in the United States today, expressed similar feelings about Omi fifty-four years later.

> ... The major thought on my mind, now that my mind has actually absorbed the loss in my life of Dr. Wehl, may the Almighty rest her soul, is what a gift her life was to me, and to absolutely every one who was blessed to know her. Such a brain she had! To know thousands of people, to remember details of their lives, to help them through illness, and the stress it causes. And, of course, to help them to know and understand their children's development.
>
> The concern that Dr. Wehl showed for each person was legendary — but true. How many times, I ask myself, did she call just as I was finishing my examination — to share what she knew, and to get to the bottom of the course of treatment? No hello, no goodbye. Just pure doctoring. What she must have gone through to become a physician. The years that preceded her coming to New York. Her life as the most adoring of mothers, the most cherishing wife, the most respectful Jewish daughter. How did she manage to convey her love for her grandchildren without a word — was it her eyes, or her touch?
>
> I did find myself unable to write even one story down. I can not even give one example of her gift, her genius. How could I possibly choose? Surely she taught us all of what the human spirit is capable,

if only we are able to implement the Almighty's way. Oh, how I miss her. And, although it still brings tears to my eyes, I love remembering a hundred-and-one things about my relationship with her and with her dear family. How grateful I am to have had a small role in her wonderful life.

Two other outstanding specialists sent in their tributes to Omi:

Dr. Bertram Cohn, Chief of Pediatric Surgery at Maimonides Hospital, wrote this tribute to Omi:

Dr. Selma Wehl had a commitment. She gave excellence. She demanded excellence.

Her patients and their families came first. Only the best would do. She had no sympathy for a delay in the Emergency Room. She would be on the phone and insist that her patient not be kept waiting. If there was an emergency, no wait was to be tolerated. Care was needed NOW.

If an illness was complex, she insisted on additional help and consultation. If one consultant could not clarify and solve the entire problem quickly and immediately, others would be called. On one occasion she had a patient with a complex and serious neurologic problem. Dr. Wehl immediately called in the Director of Pediatrics and the Chief of Pediatric Neurology. Most pediatricians would have been satisfied with these opinions but not Dr. Wehl. Her patient was still very ill and there had been no immediate response to the treatment. She was satisfied only when she had called in the Chief of Infectious Diseases of the City Health Department and kept after him until he came to the bedside and examined her patient and assured her that everything was in order. Until that point, she was not satisfied. She kept calling all the doctors involved to be sure that every test had been done and every report checked. Everything had to be NOW.

This demand for excellence often led to a question. Was she too involved? Was she acting more like a relative, a grandmother? But the parents of her patients knew she was both doctor and relative. She could not set limits on trying to help her patients. She was involved totally and committed totally. Her energy was unusual. As long as there was a problem to be solved she was on the phone, discussing, planning, and carrying out what had to be done. It could be midnight or five a.m. She did not know the meaning of a nine-to-five day.

Her goal was to get the very best for the patient. If the specialist needed was in another borough or another city, she was the first to insist that the patient be sent to that physician.

As a young person in Europe she showed exceptional intellect and determination. She studied hard and graduated not only from medical school but even became a specialist in pediatrics at a time when such an achievement was not easy for a religious Jewish woman. When she was forced to leave and come to the United States she worked again with great determination as a paramedical helper until it was possible for her to have her credentials recognized. Again, with hard work and determination, she established herself in Boro Park as an outstanding physician and member of the community.

Her service to the children of the community came at a time when many of the families had just arrived from Europe and she became a bridge for many of her patients. How fortunate they were to have Dr. Wehl for their children, the same Dr. Wehl they had known in Europe. Not only were they able to obtain expert medical care and advice, but their physician had experienced the same dislocation and loss and could better understand their needs and problems.

Her example as a person was equally important. She showed a devotion to culture and education that never weakened. By example she showed how a person could re-establish a career in a new country and still hold to her views and beliefs. As a woman she raised a family to be proud of and who carry on her values into future generations.

Indeed her life was unusual. She achieved high education and respect at a time when the obstacles were enormous. Her influence spanned two continents and many generations. She worked at her chosen profession for a full lifetime with the blessing of a mind that was crystal-clear until the very last moment.

As an individual who demanded the very best from all around her she placed even greater demands on herself. Loved and respected by all who knew her, her impact was beyond measure. Selma Wehl achieved what she set out to do and did it well. She was indeed a woman of valor.

Dr. Irving Fish, Chief Pediatric Neurologist at New York University Hospital, wrote:

In April 1977, my secretary told me I had a telephone call from a doctor in Brooklyn. As a pediatric neurologist this is not a very unusual thing. I get many such calls every day. What followed, however, was unusual. It was my first contact with Dr. Wehl. She was calling to ask me about a patient with an attack of unconsciousness. Her voice was that of an older woman, and when she told me the story of this child I knew I was talking to someone special. Dr. Wehl described the symptoms quickly and accurately and gave me, in a few words, the entire history of the patient. It was as if this was her only patient. "You will see the patient today, Dr. Fish." I could not say no. This was the first of many phone calls from Dr. Wehl. And always, she spoke about the the patient as if it was the only patient she had. And after I saw the patient, I could be sure of a phone call within a few minutes. "So, Dr. Fish, what do you think?" It became clear that these were not her patients, these were her children; in fact, these were family. She cared for them, she encouraged them, she scolded them — loved them. And it showed! She understood not only their physical problems but how those problems impacted upon the entire family. She never hesitated to call me about her patients because she loved them, and because she loved them she wanted the best for them.

One day, one of her families came in to see me. They told me, "Dr. Wehl's husband died last week."

"That is too bad, was he a sick man?" I said.

"He was ninety-five years old," the patient said. "Do you know how old she is?"

"No."

"She is in her eighties."

I was shocked. I realized that after the first phone call I never thought how old Dr. Wehl was, and because of the obvious large size of her practice, I figured her to be a woman in her fifties or early sixties at the most. How could a woman in her eighties be so up to date in her medical knowledge? How could a woman in her eighties have the memory she had? How could a woman in her eighties work as many hours as she did?

I work hard. But I cannot begin to tell you how many mornings before I went to work and how many evenings after I came home from work, she called me from her office. "Dr. Fish, I have a little girl here ... " One summer evening about nine o'clock, she called me about a patient. We discussed the patient and then she said to me "You know, Dr. Fish, I am tired."

"Take a vacation," I said. "You are working too hard."

Imagine a woman in her late eighties working six days a week, working fourteen to sixteen hours a day, handling with exquisite care very difficult problems, on her feet, children crying, telling me in a rather surprised voice, "I am tired."

Who is this woman? I said to myself. I must go and meet her. The next time I spoke to her I suggested that I come over to her office and meet her. "Good, bring your wife, we will have a cup of tea." However, every time I suggested a time that we meet, she had another reason not to meet. "I am busy. You are busy The holidays are coming."

When I heard that she died I was very upset — upset that she died, and upset that I never had a chance to meet her in person. But later on, thinking about it, maybe, once again Dr. Wehl was right. I am told that she was a small woman who at the end walked slowly. That is wrong. To me Dr. Wehl is a giant, who stands emotionally and intelligently tall, honest and firm. She is an imposing individual who I feel very privileged to have known and who has constantly inspired me to do my best for my patients.

Dr. Wehl called me many times. At the end of the conversation she never said goodbye. I am glad she didn't.

May she rest in peace!

CHAPTER 15

The End of an Era

"Oh, Mrs. H., I just want one more year."

hen my baby was born ten months ago, Dr. Wehl came to visit me in the hospital. She said, 'I brought you something that I hope will last.' She brought me a little white wicker cradle with little silk flowers. On previous occasions she had sent me balloons. She explained, 'Balloons don't last; now I hope you will have something that lasts.' I am so happy she brought me that little basket. I do hope it will last. I have it in a special place; I cherish it so. I guess Dr. Wehl knew something that nobody knew, because at the beginning of the year she said, 'Oh, Mrs. H., I just want one more year.' "

In reality Omi spoke to us many times about retiring this July but we all knew that medicine was her life and that retirement for her would be a life without meaning. We had no real indication of any major illness; death came almost suddenly to Omi. She was a woman who, in the words of Rabbi Gershon Weiss, "had gone through the trials and tribulations of life, during Germany's *haskalah* (enlightenment) period, who could have had any excuse to desecrate the Shabbos." Rabbi Weiss elaborated, "Do you know anybody who spent an entire day doing *mitzvos*? Dr. Wehl did. Her entire life, eighty-eight years or more, כֻּלוֹ חֶסֶד כֻּלוֹ הַטָבָה, *completely doing good to others*." This life was now coming to an end.

Despite the fact that we had no concrete forewarnings of this darkness descending upon the world, we did have certain signs from Heaven. Prior to Omi's demise, an intimate member of the family had two remarkable dreams. The first one portrayed a casket, carried by eight angels in white, being brought to Opi . . . When the casket was opened, it was Omi who was inside. A single dream by itself can be a mere fantasy, but a second dream followed. This next dream occurred three days before the dreadful event transpired. In it, all the details of the funeral were given. The second dream, dreamt by the same person, turned out to be one hundred percent accurate to the minutest detail. We feel that the second dream's accuracy can be interpreted as an indication of the validity of the first one.

Omi's last days were no different from the months and years that preceded them. She was able to carry out her mission to the very end of her life. As a patient wrote: "I spoke to her in the morning and asked her about bringing my five-month-old son in for his injection. She was not feeling well, but, nevertheless, told me to bring him in that afternoon." The appointment was subsequently canceled and rescheduled for a future date. The cancellation of office appointments was necessitated by Omi's going to the hospital for a chest x-ray. The x-ray showed no evidence of a bronchial infection. While waiting for her turn at the hospital, Omi was greeted by many of her colleagues who happened by. In retrospect, it was their farewell to her.

That evening, at nine-thirty, Omi still spoke to a patient, the daughter of Rabbi Meir Stern, the *rosh yeshivah* of Passaic. This would be the last piece of medical advice that she was to give. At two-thirty in the morning, on the third day of Nissan 5747, April 2, 1987, after speaking to members of the family, her great *neshamah* (soul) left her.

Omi went to her eternal life, peacefully and at rest. It was hard to believe that Hashem's emissary, who had brought life to so many others, was gone; her candle of light had been snuffed out.

As the news spread through Boro Park, the tremors of the shock began to hit. The funeral attracted thousands of people. The 'little lady' who had come to Boro Park with 'three strikes against her' left in royal fashion. A police escort, extending to the outskirts of Boro Park, accompanied her departure.

To an extent Omi's life was like a book from which we all can learn. Rabbi Yaakov Pollak eloquently stated the following words of inspiration at her funeral. "Somehow we compared Dr. Wehl to the *karban tamid* (daily sacrifice). We always thought that Boro Park would be here forever, and all the institutions of Boro Park would be here forever and Dr. Wehl would be here forever. She was an institution, a rather rare institution; a rare individual ... There are three Talmudic views as to what constitutes the *klal gadol b'Torah* (overriding Torah principle): (1) love of your fellow man, (2) the book of the history of man, (3) the daily sacrifice.

"Somehow Dr. Wehl incorporated all these aspects into her being. Her love for her fellow man; the mere presence of so many of her friends here today bears fine testimony to the love she had for her fellow man. I think each and every one of you can write books about the self-sacrifice that she displayed in carrying out, I won't say of her profession, but her love to *Yisrael*. Self-sacrifice not only as a doctor, but as a Jewess ... Her life was a story, a book of a *mentsch*. What a beautiful book it was, despite the many difficulties that she encountered. She came to these shores running away from persecution, not knowing what she would find here. Luckily, she had a profession ... the third view, namely the *karban tamid*. She was this *karban tamid*. 'This is the burnt offering which you should bring unto Hashem every day ... The lamb you shall offer, one in the morning — and the second lamb you shall offer between the two eventides.' Imagine still two days ago seeing patients in the office; imagine talking to a patient last night at nine-thirty with her full faculties. Imagine last night, at one-thirty a.m., still conversing with her daughter-in-law ... the same self-sacrifice, the same sanctity, the same intensity and devotion that existed in the morning period of her life existed at the twilight years."

A seemingly remarkable incident occurred at the cemetery. For no apparent reason the casket was unable to be lowered into the grave. A woman of Omi's physical stature should certainly not have created any such problem. Yet the opening of the grave was too small; it had to be widened. A number of our people took shovels and proceeded to perform the *mitzvah*. Thus, not only was the grave closed by strictly observant Jews, but even the opening had to be completed by those who observed the Torah and its commandments.

The *shivah* and *sheloshim* period brought with them recollections of hundreds and thousands of incidents of Omi's *chesed* and medical expertise. Everyone had their own stories to tell. It was no wonder that the auditorium of Bais Yaakov of Boro Park was filled with

throngs of people as the *sheloshim* period came to an end. At that time Rabbis and other leaders of the generations had the opportunity to eulogize Omi in an appropriate manner. According to the Matesdorfer Rav, "She achieved the highest level of being a messenger of the Almighty." Indeed it is our feeling that part of the aspect of being a loyal messenger is that one develops common characteristics with the One she serves. The seal of Hashem is truthfulness. Omi did her job in a most honest and truthful way. Thus she was privileged to become His agent. As a patient wrote, "Just as the loss of a *gadol b'Torah*, her existence as a role model is irreplaceable."

It has been suggested that future generations would benefit from reading about this legend. The question was not whether a book should be written, but rather how it would be possible to limit its size and scope. If all of us who worked on this book, the authors, the editors, the publishers, friends and patients have accomplished this, we are indebted to the Almighty.

A patient wrote: "Her mission is not complete. Her life's work, her joy for medicine, her wish that *klal yisrael* be healthy still carries on in *Gan Eden*, where Dr. Wehl is a *melitzah yesharah* and we hope as always that her diagnosis for blessings and success will be accepted in front of the Heavenly throne."

Innocent little children often express their feelings simply and clearly. Two little girls, attending Bnos Zion of Bobov, after hearing of the *petirah* of Omi addressed each other, the younger one asking the older one, "What do we do now? Dr. Wehl is no longer here." The older one replied, "We can go to her grave and *daven*, and Hashem will accept our prayers, and then no one will get sick anymore."

AN APPRECIATION

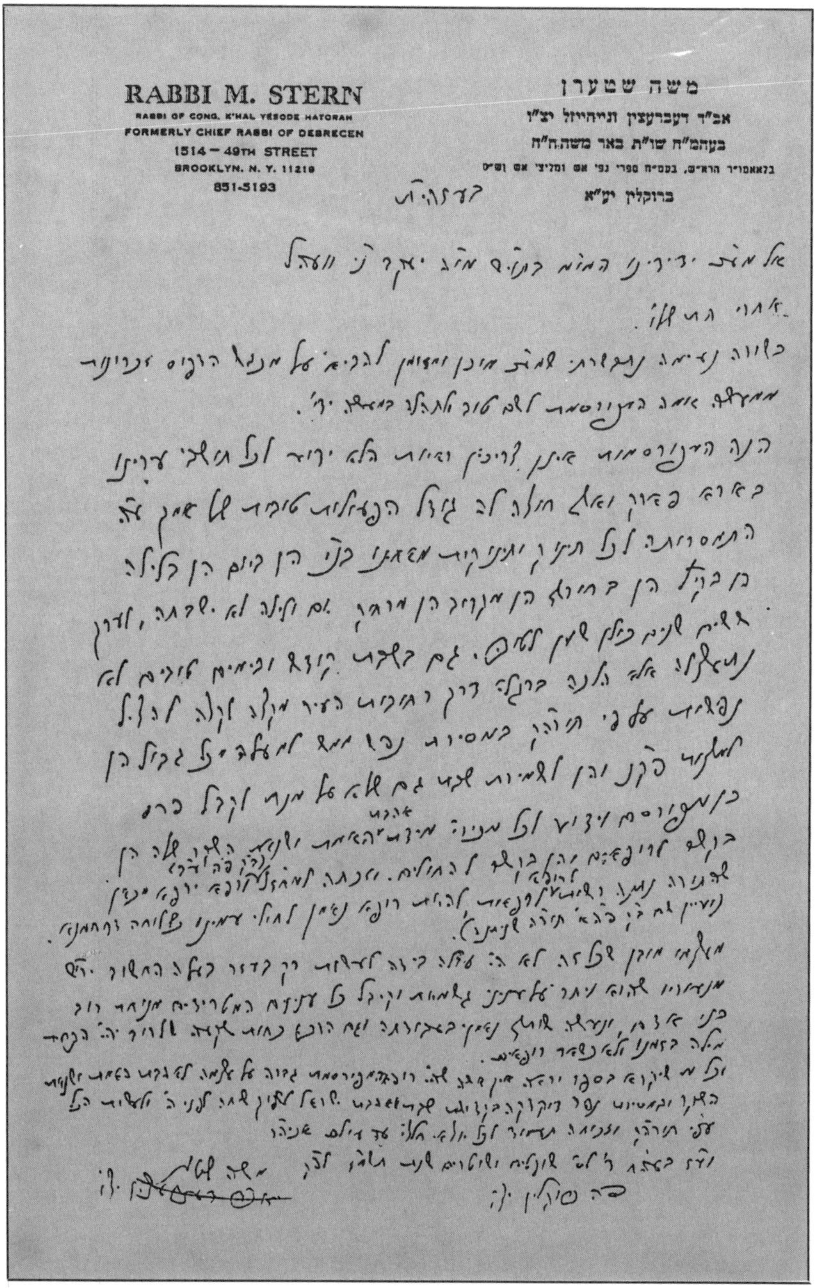

RABBI M. STERN
RABBI OF CONG. K'HAL YESODE HATORAH
FORMERLY CHIEF RABBI OF DEBRECEN
1514 — 49TH STREET
BROOKLYN, N. Y. 11219
851-5193

משה שטערן
אב"ד דעברעצין תויחויזל יצ"ו
בעהמ"ח שו"ת באר משה ח"ח
בלאאמו"ר הרא"ם, בעמ"ח ספרי נפי אש ומליצי אש וש"ס
ברוקלין יע"א

AN APPRECIATION

by Rabbi Yeruchem Olshin,
Rosh HaYeshivah, Beth Medrash Govoha, Lakewood, N.J.

This volume is part of
THE ARTSCROLL SERIES®
an ongoing project of
translations, commentaries and expositions
on Scripture, Mishnah, liturgy, history,
the classic Rabbinic Writings,
biographies, and thought.

For a brochure of current publications
visit your local Hebrew bookseller
or contact the publisher:

Mesorah Publications, Ltd.

1969 Coney Island Avenue
Brooklyn, New York 11223
(718) 339-1700